Hacking Reality

UPGRADE YOUR LIFE FROM THE INSIDE OUT

Rob Nelson, MS

Taproots Press

Sebastopol, California

Hacking Reality
Upgrade Your Life from the Inside Out

Cover image "Heart" by Krista Lynn Brown © 2009
www.DevaLuna.com

Printed in the United States of America

First Printing, 2019

ISBN 978-1-7336826-0-2

Taproots Press
PO Box 1119
Sebastopol, CA 95472

www.TaprootsPress.com

Contents

Why This Book? 1

Part 1: 7

Questioning Reality 9

Horror Films 17

That's Entertainment 23

Putting Psyche Back into Psychology..29

You Are a Soul..35

Playing by the Rules 43

The Myth of Materialism 47

Leveraging Quantum Weirdness 55

Stepping into Parallel Universes 63

Morphic Fields..69

The Fields That Make You You..77

Epigenetics: Hacking Your Genes 83

The Subconscious Mind 89

Fight or Flight 97

The Freeze Response 103

The Trauma Capsule 107

Reenactment..113

Your Younger Self is Real 117

Why Do We Struggle? 123

Reverse Engineering 131

Part II 137

EFT Crash Course 139

Going for the Jugular 147

The Paradox of Helping 153

Working with Others in the Matrix 159

Past Life Resolution 167

I See Dead People...175

Meetings with Remarkable Spirits............................181

What Would You Like? 187

Meeting Your Future Self..193

Part III..199

Your Body is Not a Machine 201

Hacking the Reality of Physical Issues 205

Healing in the Field 213

Autoimmune Disorders 219

Cancer 225

The Parent Child Relationship 233

Romantic Relationships 239

Procrastination 247

Hacking Reality for Others.......................................253

Hacking Your Money Mindset...................................261

Conclusion..271

Resources 275

Index 278

*This book is dedicated to my beloved wife and soul mate
Krista Lynn Brown, my daughters India and Eden,
and all the wonderful clients and students who've helped
me access such profound levels of healing.*

*Special acknowledgments to Gary Craig and Karl Dawson for
their world-changing work and inspiring generosity of spirit,
my big sister Andrea Asebedo, who first introduced me to
metaphysical reality, my early mentors Steve Shirrell,
Lin Eucalyptus, & Bev Shoopman, my absolutely brilliant
editor Sarah Grace Powers, and the incredible Launch Crew
who helped this book become a reality, and last but not least,
my loving parents Bob & Shirley Nelson.*

Important Disclaimer

Rob Nelson is not a doctor or licensed health care practitioner of any kind. The information in this book is provided for educational purposes only, and it is not intended to substitute for medical, psychiatric or psychological advice. Please consult a doctor or qualified health care practitioner for any medical, emotional or psychological problems and especially before discontinuing any medications. Reading this book in no way constitutes a client-practitioner relationship between the reader and Rob Nelson. Please take full responsibility for your own health and well-being while reading this book.

Hacking Reality

UPGRADE YOUR LIFE FROM THE INSIDE OUT

Figure 1: Artist Unknown

Why This Book?

Would you like to live a more satisfying, authentic life? To stop holding yourself back, step out of old patterns and let go of your tired old story? Are you brave enough to step out of the dull, stuffy box of conventional reality and take a look around? If your answer is yes, I wrote this book for you!

Most self-help books offer sensible advice for improving yourself by managing your time more efficiently, cultivating a positive attitude, and adopting better habits. Given enough time, will power and self-discipline, I'm sure that sort of stuff can really work for you. Then again, here we are.

Personally, I'm busy as hell most of the time and I tend to be impatient. And my will power and self-discipline seem to wax and wane with the Moon. I prefer a more *non-sensible* approach to change. One that leverages cutting-edge breakthroughs in physics, epigenetics, and psychology.

To put it another way, the usual self-help advice is really all about having a better adjustment to reality. How about we adjust reality instead? At least the way you experience it. 'Losing touch with reality' generally means going crazy, but don't worry. This book is about getting *more* in touch with reality, and that makes upgrading your life a heck of a lot easier.

I've got a really cool job. For the last twelve years, I've been privileged to witness healing miracles on a fairly routine basis. Miracles, not in the religious sense of supernatural intervention, but rather changes that defy our common expectations of what's possible. My job is to facilitate those kinds of experiences for my clients –

changes in health, relationships, self-expression, prosperity, inner peace, you name it.

I'm able to pull this off on a pretty consistent basis. Not because I have any sort of special magical powers. I'm just a regular guy. But I *have* developed a somewhat unconventional perspective on reality that opens up new possibilities. I've also been lucky enough to master certain change-work tools that make 'impossible' things not only possible but relatively easy to manifest.

Hacking Reality is about sharing those wonderful tools with you, along with certain alternative perspectives. This is all very learnable stuff. If I can pull off miracles, so can you.

Here's the Plan

This book is presented in three sections. We'll start off in Part I by taking a look at how our default settings for certain key aspects of 'reality' might be a bit outdated or just plain wrong. Our explorations will range from scientific topics like quantum physics, epigenetics, morphic fields, and the fight/flight/freeze response, to more esoteric matters such as psychology, the human soul, and the meaning of life.

Once we've established a more miracle-friendly foundation, Part II will introduce you to the incredibly powerful change-work tools I use, EFT (Emotional Freedom Techniques, aka meridian tapping) and Matrix Reimprinting.

I've designed a crash course in EFT for you, and just this alone will transform your life. We'll explore ways of using EFT, including the state-of-the-art change work tool Matrix Reimprinting. Matrix isn't so much a self-help tool, but understanding the concepts and principles is totally empowering and will massively leverage your effectiveness with EFT.

With EFT and Matrix Reimprinting in your tool belt, Part III will explore some of the life issues that challenge or bedevil us, including money, relationships, weight issues, physical problems like cancer, autoimmune disease and chronic pain, blocks to success and procrastination, and new ways to help struggling friends and family.

For the last eight years, I've taught hundreds of students how to do the kind of work that I do, basically teaching the same damn curriculum over and over again. You might think that would get kind of boring. It never does! My students tend to be brilliant, wise, compassionate, creative healers, and each class explores the frontiers of change-work with new perspectives and insights.

This book is a distillation of what I've been teaching all these years, and what I've learned from my wonderful students. My hope is that *Hacking Reality* will open up new possibilities for you, empowering you to lead your most authentic life. If your life is kind of stuck, how about a nice, refreshing quantum leap?

What is Hacking?

According to Wikipedia hackers are:

> *Individuals who enjoy the intellectual challenge of creatively overcoming limitations of software systems to achieve novel and clever outcomes. The act of engaging in activities (such as programming) in a spirit of playfulness and exploration is termed 'hacking.' However, the defining characteristic of a hacker is not the activities performed, but the manner in which it is done and whether it is something exciting and meaningful.*

Hacking is the ability to get deep into the software code to pull off extraordinary changes. Your own personal Operating System is the software we'll be hacking in this book, the main program running your life. Your OS is a complex system of beliefs, understandings, reflexes, and triggers – code which likely contains inconsistencies, errors and perhaps a virus or two.

Why is this important? Your Operating System entirely generates your experience of life. Not just your thoughts and feelings, but also your physical health. It also orchestrates most of the events and circumstances you encounter. Incredibly, most of us are basically still running whatever OS was installed by age 7. This book is about de-bugging the thing and installing some crucial upgrades.

Let's see if we can get you some 'novel and clever outcomes' that Wikipedia mentions, and in that spirit of creativity, playfulness, and exploration. If all goes to plan, we're going to have a good time together.

You'll note that I'm writing in a conversational style. While a great deal of research went into the writing, this is not an academic or technical book. You won't find footnotes or scientific studies backing up my assertions. I'm asking you to adopt an experiential approach. Trust your own head, heart, and gut to validate the truth of this material. Try this stuff out and notice how your life begins to change!

Our Hacking Tools

EFT (sometimes called 'tapping') is a way of hacking into the non-verbal part of the brain that controls stress and *fight or flight*. It's like a form of emotional acupuncture that uses finger tapping rather than needles.

It's a deceptively simple technique on the surface. We tap on 12 key points over and over while focusing on whatever problem we want to release. I've taught basic EFT to children as young as 7 or 8 years old, but there's no limit to how deep you can go with it. The amazing thing is, it actually works! I'm excited to share this incredible tool with you.

Matrix Reimprinting is a way of using EFT within the context of a bad memory. If we were working on a memory from when you were five years old, I'd have you step into that event as you are right now and have you tap on your little 5-year-old self.

The basic idea is that sometimes a part of us splits off during a really bad event, in order to hold the overwhelming emotional intensity for us, which enables us to carry on. For us, the event becomes just a memory, but our split off younger self is trapped, endlessly reliving the scene no matter how much time has passed. With Matrix, we're able to set them free by tapping away their distress.

But we go even further by working with the younger self to change the picture to something wonderful and empowering. We reimprint that new picture through a simple process, and now we have a new, positive 'memory' that overwrites the original. We know that the original event happened, on a rational level, but looking back we see and feel that lovely new picture.

It's hard to overstate how profound this can be in upgrading our experience of life! The new picture not only changes how we feel, it also changes what we believe – our beliefs about ourselves and about life. Whatever negative decisions we made during the bad event became distorted perceptual filters. Changing the picture reverses these decisions, debugging our Operating System in a powerful way.

Matrix Reimprinting is the ultimate reality hacking tool.

Freedom to Change

About 25 years ago I experienced a powerful spiritual vision. It came to me in the middle of the night, but it was no dream. To this day I can remember parts of it vividly. This vision gave me an awareness of the freedom we all share to change our experience of life—to choose liberation from suffering.

I was shown a space of utter darkness, and within this darkness, there were islands of light. These islands of light were surrounded by Souls, much like thousands of sperm surrounding an egg. The Souls were all observing whatever little illuminated reality show was happening on their island.

Approaching one of these islands, it seemed to have a kind of carnival feel. Almost like a circus sideshow, all lit up at night and providing some sort of outlandish spectacle – an entertainment. I found myself joining in the witnessing. The other souls seemed oblivious of me and of each other. Their full attention was given to the scene unfolding before them.

I don't really remember much about the 'show,' but the feel of it was heavy – some sort of human drama and not a happy scene at all. On the contrary, it was harrowing and engrossing. The sense of bearing witness was intense.

And though it was tough to watch, I felt a kind of obligation to remain engaged in the unfolding drama – a kind of *moral* obligation. It seemed vitally important to witness what was happening.

Somehow I was participating, contributing, simply by giving it my full attention.

And then I was gently pulled away from the island and shown the greater perspective again. My 'show' was just one island among many. In fact, there were others quite nearby, and I could easily 'swim' over to them. All of them were different and interesting and possibly *much* more enjoyable than the one I'd been involved with.

That was when it really hit me. There *was* no moral virtue or obligation to stay with any particular show. None whatsoever! It was entirely my choice. And it had been my choice to become so engrossed in that one scene, that the others were forgotten. Without really intending to, I chose to forget that I had any choice.

This wonderful freedom to disengage—to choose a more pleasant, enjoyable or even ecstatic reality, this was the heart of my vision and has become the heart of my work today, all these years later. This is what I hope to share with you in *Hacking Reality*.

The Lottery Test

People generally hire me because their life sucks. It might not be *all* that bad, but they long for something greater – a deeply loving relationship, financial freedom, career success, better health, freer and more satisfying creative self-expression. Something needs to change for them to be the person they want to be.

I see my work as helping people disengage from whatever unpleasant reality they've been stuck in and take a little swim over to a *new* one that's much more inspiring and lovely. I'm pretty sure I've got the best job in the world. At least for me.

Years ago I realized that if I won the lottery – hundreds of millions of dollars – I'd still want to do this work I do. It really is that satisfying. But no matter how much I love it, I can only work with just a few people every year. Hence this book.

If you'd like *your* life to pass the lottery test, I hope that *Hacking Reality* will help get you there. Let's start this journey by taking a good hard look at reality itself in the next chapter.

Part 1:

WHAT IS REALITY?
EXPLORING YOUR DEFAULT SETTINGS

*"It is the mark of an educated mind to be able to entertain
a thought without accepting it"*
--- Aristotle

CHAPTER 1

Questioning Reality

T his is a book about hacking reality, but what exactly *is* reality? The dictionary suggests that reality is something that's real and actual, as opposed to imaginary, fictional or merely apparent. It's something that exists independently of ideas concerning it. We might have theories about the Moon, for example, which may or may not be accurate. But the Moon itself is real.

On the other hand, there's a psychological level of reality which very much determines our own experience. An astronomer and astrologer may regard the Moon in different ways. An indigenous shaman will experience the reality of the rain forest in a different way than the hedge fund manager who's just arrived for an ayahuasca ceremony. Or the geologist looking for oil reserves.

Clearly, no two people share exactly the same psychological reality. Even siblings growing up in the same family can have vastly different experiences of childhood. And objective circumstances can give us wildly different lives. My world is radically different than a coffee farmer in Vietnam. Or a corporate lobbyist in Washington, DC. Or a Baptist preacher in rural Alabama.

For the most part, *Hacking Reality* concerns de-bugging our own personal psychological reality, but it may be helpful to delve down into the nearly universal core assumptions we likely share. I think of these as the factory installed 'default settings' that are rarely examined but very much inform our fundamental reality.

Let's take a quick overview of some of our more bottom line assumptions, presented here in no particular order:

You Exist

This may be our most basic setting. Obviously you exist, or you wouldn't be reading this book, right? But what exactly *are* you? In *The Lazy Man's Guide to Enlightenment*, Thaddeus Golas wrote that being the ego consciousness of a human body is a bit like being mayor of New York City. There are a LOT of other beings involved.

Supposedly there are more bacteria in your gut than stars in the galaxy. Your body couldn't live without them, but are those bacteria you? For that matter, are your cells you? Is your heart you? Your body? And if your body *is* you, then when your body dies, do you die with it?

And if you happen to say "I'm really mad at myself," that seems to imply there are two of you! Or you might really want to lose 15 pounds, but then who is it spooning ice cream into your mouth? It's pretty clear that the word "I" is just a subset of "You" which apparently includes your subconscious mind.

And then there's the idea of having a Higher Self. When you get a flash of intuition, who or what is providing it, and if that's not you then how does it have access to your thoughts? Are you part of some greater consciousness but suffering from amnesia? Lots of questions! We'll see if we can chase down some answers as we go along.

The World is Real

Physical reality certainly *seems* real. If you throw a rock at my head, I'm definitely going to duck! Our direct, immediate experience of the world comes to us through our senses – sight, sound, taste, touch, and smell. It's very easy to assume that *only* what we perceive through these five senses is real. There can't be anything else.

I really like how actor turned philosopher Russell Brand puts it:

> *Anything we're describing through science we're describing through the prism of the five limited senses. Our eyes can only see between infrared light and ultraviolet light, there's light bouncing around everywhere. Our ears can only hear a tiny decibel range, can't hear the noise of a dog whistle, can't hear any high-pitched frequency sounds. Isn't it likely then that there*

are other vibrations, frequencies, energies, consciousness moving through the universe?

In other words, we're incredibly limited in what we can perceive, and yet we assume that's all there is. Most deaf people are well aware that sound exists, even if they themselves can't hear anything. But what if *everyone* was deaf? How would anyone actually know about sound?

Why is this relevant? There's a lot more going on in your world than meets the eye. If we can allow our sense of reality to expand beyond the purely physical we can gain access to new possibilities for change.

Time is Linear

Albert Einstein famously wrote:

For we convinced physicists, the distinction between past, present, and future is only an illusion, however persistent.

What the hell does that mean? Is Einstein suggesting that everything is happening all at the same time? That's just too much for a lot of people.

One of the starkest aspects of this reality is the aging process. We start out in the womb, we're born, grow up, hopefully have a nice long plateau, then decline in old age and eventually die. And once we die, we decompose! How can one argue against that? Also, if everything is happening at once, how is it we can remember the past but not the future?

This is deep stuff, and we'll get deeper into it later, but let me just say that Einstein was really onto something. Oddly enough, with Matrix Reimprinting time is one of the easiest things to hack! It's just a bit like time travel.

You Are Your Body

Years ago a friend sent me a really awesome shirt for Christmas. Every time I'd wear it someone would tell me how great it looked on me—I called it my lucky shirt. After 20 years though, the color faded, the collar started to fray, and one sad day it came out of the wash with huge holes in it!

I loved my lucky shirt, but it never occurred to me that I *was* that shirt. It was just something I wore. What if it's much the same with our bodies? We wear them. We inhabit them. And once they wear out, we get new ones.

We'll be exploring the implications of who we really are in this book. If you've been entirely identifying as your body, it's pretty liberating stuff.

Only Matter is Real

If you've spent any time hanging around a university, or maybe even high school, you were likely exposed to the Materialist worldview which masquerades as 'scientific.' Many adopt it as a sign of being educated and superior to the rank superstitions of religion. They do not realize that 'Materialism' is simply metaphysics and no more subject to scientific proof than belief in the Flying Spaghetti Monster.

We'll be looking at the rather grim implications of this worldview in the chapter on Materialism. It's definitely a wet blanket in terms of hacking reality – the kind of blanket they put on you at the dentist office for X-rays. Except that this one only protects you from joy and miracles.

Religious Beliefs

I once worked with a lovely woman who grew up in Kenya. Her family was some kind of fundamentalist Christian, and she absolutely believed that God was a giant white man who lived on a big throne in the sky. I asked her whether or not God had a giant penis. After some thought, she said yes, she supposed he must.

You probably think that's pretty silly stuff. My client thought so too after we tapped a bit. But this is what she'd been taught as a young child (except for the penis part) and she'd just taken it all in uncritically. She'd never taken the time to go back and examine her own beliefs—until they began to really get in her way.

Let's look at some other common religious beliefs, which might apply just as much to Buddhists as Christians. See if any of this stuff sounds familiar:

God made the world but lives outside of it. This world is a bad place where we're being schooled, tested or punished. Heaven or Nirvana or Paradise is where we really want to be, and it's not here on Earth, but somewhere else, where God lives. When we finally get there, we'll be happy forever.

And we get to heaven by following the rules. The rules are conveniently spelled out in a Holy Book, which was written by God (or by some holy man inspired by God). If we follow the rules religiously, then we've got a shot at going to Heaven when we die.

If we fail to follow the rules, we'll end up in Hell or reincarnate and suffer endlessly. This is because we're inherently bad. We're flawed or sinners or unevolved or attached. We're separate from God and need to be saved or redeemed or liberated before we're worthy.

At the risk of stepping on some toes here, I'd like to suggest that most of this stuff was fabricated, or at least distorted by religious politicians seeking power and control. It's worked pretty well for them too, in terms of disempowering and controlling the believers.

Hacking Reality is based upon metaphysics I've cobbled together over the course of my lifetime, intended to empower you and help you assume more control over your life. You don't need to believe this stuff for the book to help you, but here's a quick overview:

Alternative Metaphysics

God is immanent – meaning present in everything. There is nothing that isn't God, and nowhere God is not. In quantum physics terms, God is The Field.

God is not a person – not a He or a She. But God is every person. Every animal. Every tree. Every rock. Every planet, star, and galaxy. Everything. And therefore, everything is sacred.

Everything is one with God, including you. And you volunteered to forget that fact. Earth is a place where Souls take on a physical form to experience the illusion of being separate from God. No one actually is separate from God, ever, but it can be a very convincing illusion!

We take on our lifetime as an assignment or mission, and it's almost always a tough one. Sometimes it's incredibly difficult.

Your Soul has actually volunteered to go through many lifetimes with a somewhat different personality in each one. You are one of these many personalities, which are all evolving together. Your Soul is very great, magnificent really, and only a small part inhabits your Earthly body and personality.

Your Soul might be regarded as your Higher Self, which you can choose to connect with. Connecting with your Soul or Higher Self can really accelerate your growth and development in this lifetime.

You are supposed to be here. Volunteering to incarnate here is a great honor, in part because it requires great courage. And although our lives can be truly hellish here on Earth, you are *not* being tested or punished. You are one with God and whatever learning and experience you gain here benefits everyone. Your mission is to be you, and therefore you cannot fail.

Heaven/Nirvana is right here, right now and available to you at all times. There is nothing you need to do to earn access. No lesson to learn or test to pass to become worthy. No one cast you out of the Garden, you volunteered to forget who you really are and to forget that you forgot.

Your participation in this difficult lifetime assignment is entirely optional – you can check out at any time, and people sometimes do. However, you've gone to *a lot of trouble* getting this far. The information in this book is intended to help you complete your mission by massively accelerating your progress.

Once you really *get* the learning you came here for, it's possible to reawaken to Heaven here on Earth. It's totally okay to do so. There's actually some pretty cool stuff to do here besides all the suffering. In the meantime though, let's do start off with the suffering in the next chapter, just in case your life or the life of a loved one is a bit more on the Hellish end of the spectrum.

CHAPTER 2

Horror Films

As a kid in the sixties I totally loved monster movies – *Frankenstein*, *The Mummy*, *Creature from the Black Lagoon*. My friends and I couldn't get enough of the melodramatic bad acting, lame plot lines and cheesy special effects. We felt we were living in the Golden Age of Monster Movies.

And then it was over. Somehow our beloved monster movies disappeared, replaced by horror films. *Godzilla* and *The Wolfman* were out. *The Exorcist* and *Texas Chainsaw Massacre* were in. And I didn't like it.

These new films were all about demons or psychopathic killers. And lots of blood and gore. They had an element of supernatural and pathological creepiness that I didn't much care for. I remember seeing *Carrie* and *The Exorcist* way back in high school, and I was seriously done.

But all these years later Hollywood is still cranking 'em out, and lots of people *love love love* horror films. They eagerly await the new release of *Bride of Chucky Part 5* in 3D. They'll stand in line for hours on opening day, waving their dollars, demanding entrance to a dark room where they can witness atrocities. I've often wondered what the hell is wrong with these people.

Just for fun, imagine I'm the sort of person who wants to improve society – a social reformer! Not only do I personally hate horror films, I firmly believe they're harmful, and *no one* should see them. In fact, they shouldn't even be made in the first place.

So I hatch a plan. On the opening day of the next big slasher flick, I'll infiltrate the theater and interrupt the film! I'll climb up in front of the screen with a megaphone and announce, "Hey, you shouldn't be here. This movie is bad for you! Movies like this are bad for society! There are other films you could see here. Please exit this theater and go watch a romantic comedy or maybe a documentary! You have other choices!"

No doubt everyone would thank me and eagerly get up to leave. It simply hadn't occurred to them that horror films might be harmful. I'm sure they'd be grateful for my intervention, motivated as it was by loving kindness. They'd probably cheer and throw me kisses.

Or maybe not.

Everyone in that audience knew full well what they were paying for. They went to some trouble to be there. Would they appreciate my good intentions? Not likely. Instead of cheers, they might be more inclined to yell rude things. Instead of kisses, they might throw other things at me!

Honestly, could you blame them? Who am I to say horror films are bad for them? For all I know watching *Saw 3* might be therapeutic for some people. Maybe it helps discharge some childhood trauma or prevents them from acting out some terrible inner violence. I rather doubt it, but can we ever truly know what's right for another human being?

The reason I'm bringing this up is that some of us seem to choose a horror film lifetime. I've heard stories from clients so appalling I've never shared them with anyone – truly the stuff of nightmares. But probably most of us have had at least a few horrific events at some point in our life. In order to help my clients, I've had to wrestle with this darker aspect of reality.

I've been helped so much by this powerful reminder from *The Lazy Man's Guide to Enlightenment* – "I wouldn't deny that experience to the One Mind."

Actually, I totally would! In the old days my default setting used to be "Oh hell no!" and still is sometimes. And I don't think unique to me. Denial, dissociation, rejection, and condemnation are all standard reactions to the horror of life. Unfortunately, they lead to repetition rather than healing and resolution. Let's continue on with our movie metaphor and see where it takes us.

Lifetimes

Have you ever gone to see a movie and it was *so* good, *so* engrossing that you really got lost in it? Sometimes we forget we're actually sitting in a chair in a dark room full of strangers. It's amazing how we can lose track of our surroundings and get swept up into the story. It's like we're really there, living through it along with the characters in the film.

No matter how engrossing it is though, no matter how beautiful, horrifying, gut-wrenching or poignant, some part of us knows it's just a movie. It's going to be over at some point. The house lights will come back on, and we'll look around and maybe shake our head. We'll find the exit and go home to our real life. The sun might still be shining when we walk out of the theater. I believe that our lifetimes are very much like this.

I first encountered this movie metaphor when I was 15 when my wonderful sister gave me a copy of Richard Bach's *Illusions*. Richard's teacher in the book, the reluctant messiah Donald Shimoda, suggests that people go see movies for two main reasons: Education and Entertainment. And really our lifetimes are no different.

Our Souls between lifetimes plan out these grand adventures and sign up to go through them with friends and loved ones. "You were my uncle last time, how about I'll be your dad in this one?" Or, "Hey, things are going to be really dark after my breakup when I'm 37, maybe you could be a random stranger who cheers me up."

I have heard that very young Souls sometimes plunge heedlessly into new lifetimes without any forethought, caught up in passion or enthusiasm. But most of us plan out all of the plot lines and important encounters well before we start merging with our body in the womb.

This notion resolves the age-old dilemma of fate vs. free will. We set up these lifetimes of our own free will and then forget all about it.

We do like surprises! Without this amnesia, there'd be no suspense. For the movie to seem real, the house lights have to dim.

So, amnesia is actually the price of admission to this reality show here on Earth. Amnesia gives us the illusion of fate, that random 'shit happens' experience. But we really do have free will. We can shake off the illusion and remember who we really are at any time we like. And that's totally okay to do! Awakening is one of the more amazing experiences we can have here on Earth, especially when we're in horror show territory.

In this process of waking up some of us go from being an extra in someone else's production to finally playing the lead role in our own movie. And, ultimately we can be the director. We can yell "Cut!" and order re-writes to the plot. We're even free to put in a happy ending if we like, Hollywood style. But this requires waking up. Otherwise, the script is set.

Volunteers

Over the years I've worked with clients who signed up for *truly* horrific movies, born into war zones or suffering horrendous abuse at the hands of parents who were criminally insane and seemingly dedicated to destroying the soul of their own child.

I believe that all of us are brave volunteers. Earth is a venue that seems a little more weighted toward Education versus Entertainment lifetimes. My clients suffering from nightmare childhoods seem *super extra* brave to me. I honor them. But, no matter how harrowing the movie, the house lights always come back on at the end and we go home.

I don't believe anyone is here to be punished. I'm absolutely certain of this. No one is forced to come here. We choose to experience both sides of every social equation – master/slave, mother/daughter, victim/perpetrator, teacher/student. These are the karmic wheels that keep us coming back for more. But we can step off the ride whenever we like. There's a simple 'cheat code' for this – love and acceptance.

Why do people have to suffer? Why does an innocent little baby have to die of thirst in the desert in Sudan? Isn't that proof that there is no God? Why do reprehensible tyrants live in luxury while good-hearted people suffer abject poverty? Isn't that proof that there's no justice? That the Universe is a cruel, uncaring place? Well, no. Not if we're *choosing* our lifetimes before we're born.

Why would a Soul choose to die in agony as a child from bone cancer? Why would a Soul choose to go through the horrendous experience of being that child's loving parent? There might be a lot of reasons, but I believe that from the Soul's perspective, having a lifetime really is like our going to see a movie. It doesn't seem real until we're in it. From their point of view, it's over in a flash, really. So what's the big fuss?

I guess finding out what all the fuss is about is part of our education here. And once we 'get it' we can move on to more entertaining aspects of reality.

In Michael Newton's *Journey of Souls*, he suggests that only a part of our Soul actually incarnates in any given lifetime. This world isn't real enough to hold all of who we are. It's not our true home, and we really have to *squeeze* into these physical bodies and personalities.

That's why dying is such a vast relief. I've heard it compared to leaving a crowded, stuffy room – opening the door to step outside into fresh air and sunshine. Or taking off a pair of tight shoes after a long day standing on your feet and walking in the cool grass.

Happily, dying isn't the *only* way to get some relief.

Ushers

Getting back to our movie theater analogy... Imagine you're in a dark theater packed with people and you're *really* not enjoying the film. In fact, you're really hating it and want to get the hell out of there, but how?

You're in luck! Ushers are standing by. Look for the red cap and jacket with brass buttons and gold piping. And they have flashlights! No need to turn on the house lights just yet. They can help you find an exit. Can you picture that?

I realized some years ago that that's *my* job. I'm an Usher. I'm here to help you find a more enjoyable movie.

There are a lot of us these days. Which is great because more and more 'moviegoers' are starting to get restless. Each new blockbuster in the Consensus Reality Theater seems a bit more dystopian – not a happy ending in sight.

So, people want out. *Where's the exit? Get me out of here!*

That's where I come in, and many more like me, flashlights at the ready. We don't come unless we're called, though. People go to a lot of trouble to be here, and it wouldn't be fair to interrupt their movie unless they ask us to.

If you've read this far, I'm guessing you're at least looking around to see where the exits might be. That's great! Having options is nice. *Hacking Reality* is my attempt to loan you a flashlight.

CHAPTER 3

That's Entertainment

D o you remember as a child, the joy of school letting out for the summer holidays? What a glorious feeling that was. If we really *do* choose our lifetimes mainly for education and entertainment, wouldn't it be wonderful if we could 'test out' of whatever lessons we're supposed to be learning here and get on with the fun stuff? How about an Endless Summer?

Because being on Earth really does offer some spectacular opportunities for enjoyment and entertainment! The horror show really is only one option - there are countless unique and wonderful experiences on offer here, possibly found nowhere else in this great big Universe.

Over the years I've worked with any number of clients whose lives were so overwhelmingly grim, they'd entirely lost their sense of wonder and fun. If that's been your experience, this chapter is for you! Pleasure and joy can be enormously healing.

At the same time, one or more of life's pleasures may have been specifically ruined for you. Sexuality contaminated by shame, enjoying food by the anxiety of body image, altered state by addiction, and so on. If that's the case, take heart. We have these new tools at hand, and it's absolutely possible to resolve our wounds and reclaim these treasures of enjoyment. So, this chapter is for you, too!

On the other hand, if you read through this menu of wonderful options and they all seem so familiar as to be obvious, let me invite you to count your blessings and bask in the warm glow of gratitude.

Here, in no particular order, are some of the Earthly Delights available to all of us.

Food & Drink

Many people mainly just 'eat to live.' But food can be *amazing* and 'living to eat' is a viable option at just about any income level. Pad Thai from a street vendor in Bangkok, or tacos and beer from a food truck can be every bit as ecstatic as a gourmet meal at a five-star restaurant.

Imagine homemade bread hot from a wood-fired oven slathered with really good butter. Or the most beautiful salad with delicate pea shoots and tomatoes ripe from the vine. How about a big ice cream cone or strawberry rhubarb pie? Picking ripe blackberries on a hot summer afternoon. In my town, we have incredible food – Indian and Sushi, Ethiopian and Italian. And people come from all over the world to sample the wine here.

You just can't get this stuff on the Astral Plane.

Sex

And then there's sex. Whoa.

Granted, if we're still reeling from traumatic sexual abuse or stuck in a passionless marriage, it can take a fair bit of work to clear the decks and hit the reset button with sex. But we've got these nearly hairless monkey bodies, totally *overloaded* with exquisite nerve endings and wild hormones. Here we can experience Duality in a very up close and personal way.

Or not. We don't even need a partner to access ecstatic sensual bliss. But of course, throwing a willing participant into the mix can really expand the possibilities. It's true that sex provides a potential venue for some of our most hellish suffering, but I have a feeling that Earth is even more famous in the spirit realm for the human sexual pleasures on offer. And inhabiting a physical body is pretty much required.

Romantic Love

Right up there with great sex is the rosy pink bubble of falling in love. That sense of the rest of the world falling away and it's just you and your beloved, SEEING each other, delighting in each other, utterly consumed by the experience. It's such a powerful ride!

If you think about it, the rosy pink bubble of romantic love can really only happen within the context of feeling alone and isolated – one of our existential default settings here on Earth. It's the contrast that makes our newfound togetherness so special, so magical. The overwhelming *relief* from loneliness. The sudden, wonderful sense of being seen and cherished. What a rush!

Physical Pleasures

Sex can be pretty incredible, but it's definitely not the only venue for physical pleasure. Getting a really great massage can be heaven. Swimming, running, swinging on a swing, playing Frisbee, climbing a tree or climbing a mountain can put us in a state of bliss.

Dancing – there are so many different kinds! Smelling a flower, feeling sunlight on your face, holding a newborn baby. Listening to the comforting sound of crickets on a warm evening. Diving into a cold river or soaking in a hot bathtub with candles lit. All of these things require a body. The good news is, if you're reading this book right now you've already got one.

Adventure

Mr. Bilbo Baggins wasn't keen on adventures, but a great many people *love* them. They're extremely entertaining! You might backpack across Europe, or take a road trip across Iceland. There's skydiving, scuba diving, whitewater rafting, mountain climbing, and trekking through the Amazon.

For some of us, just going to a club to meet new people totally qualifies, or taking a cooking class in Thailand, signing up for yoga classes, or planting our first garden. There are so many kinds of adventures, but mostly they share a certain element of surprise, suspense, risk, and potential danger, at least to some extent.

Seriously, it's not much of an adventure if you know the outcome ahead of time and if you feel totally safe throughout. Thanks to our amnesia about who we really are and the illusion of linear time, we've got all the right ingredients for our whole life to be an adventure!

Altered States

One of the most popular adventures these days is the Altered States of Consciousness Ride. There are many options, from alcohol to ayahuasca, opioids to amphetamines. Pretty much all substances are pure entertainment, in the beginning.

For many people alcohol and marijuana provide a wonderful experience, enhancing social relations and sensual pleasures. Entheogens, like shrooms, LSD, peyote, DMT and Ecstasy can offer surges of spiritual awakening with relatively gentle landings.

But every substance can be problematic when we become dependent on it. Opioids, amphetamines, and alcohol are especially ripe for abuse. The Altered States Ride can take a really nasty turn, featuring a long downhill slide into pain, loss of integrity, degradation, and some very educational suffering!

Happily, a much gentler version of the ride is available which uses meditation and yoga rather than relying on substances. Simply awakening from the illusions of this world can be a wonderful kind of rush.

Connection with Others

One of the great pleasures available to us is the sense of being part of a family or circle of friends or comrades. For some of us, this might be just one or two close friends, our partner, or perhaps an animal companion.

Being seen, valued and included. Taking part in a group endeavor. The safety of going out into the world to have fun with your posse. Feeling relaxed enough to speak your mind or heart unguardedly, spontaneously and laughing together. Sharing a deeply meaningful moment with even one other person.

Many people I work with have really missed out on this, but the amazing thing is, even after a lifetime of unwanted solitude, new friends and 'family' can show up. It happens!

Creativity

I read once that art is the decoration of space, while music is the decoration of time. Lucky for us Earth is all about space and time! The opportunity to express yourself by creating something uniquely you – a painting, a poem, a dance, a song, a play, a joke or even a self-help book – perhaps this is available on other planes of existence, but I have to believe our particular circumstances here on Earth make creativity exquisitely special.

And we're able to discover, witness and appreciate vast cultural riches created by creative geniuses over thousands of years. It's absolutely mind-blowing. And ongoing! The garage band down the street may just be the next Beatles. And check out the art-cars and installations from Burning Man sometime!

My hope is that *Hacking Reality* will help unleash your own creativity. You don't need to paint a painting or write a song, your life is your greatest creation.

Nature

Surely there's no greater masterpiece of creation than Nature herself. That old cliché, 'stop and smell the roses' is so right on. Slow down and become aware, using all of your senses. Practice tuning into the miracle of Nature unfolding all around you, even if you live in the city. We can re-enter the state of awe we once knew as children, in the presence of something ancient and brand new, humble yet utterly magnificent.

Taking in a beautiful sunset, tuning into the beauty of a gnarled old tree, exploring desert wildness and lush mountain meadows, spying a fox cavorting in the tall grass, plunging into the current of a wild river, sitting by an aromatic campfire, or just walking along a white sand beach with the waves rolling in – these have been some of the greatest pleasures in my own life.

This is just a partial list of entertainment options here on Earth – there are just so many wonderful things to do and see here, besides all of that suffering. These experiences can really feed our souls. Assuming we have souls. Do we? Perhaps we'd better take a look at that question in the next chapter.

CHAPTER 4

Putting Psyche Back into Psychology

The morning of my 36th birthday I joined my sister and her husband, my wife and several others around my father's bedside as he lay unconscious and dying, letting go of life. With each long, slow exhale we all wondered 'was that it? Was that his last breath?'

This went on for hours.

He'd stopped eating days earlier, and Hospice had switched his pain medication to morphine, allowing him to gently slip away. It was July in Redding, California – a very hot place, but that morning was cool, and we had the window open. Rolling thunder rumbled from a sky laden with dark storm clouds.

When my father finally let go of his last breath, everyone in the room felt him leave his body. There was no question at all. The air brightened, a breeze blew into the room, there was a rumble of thunder, and he was gone. He always did have a flair for the dramatic.

The field of psychology began as the study of the human Soul. The name derives from the Greek word Psyche, which translates as both soul and breath. I read once that in the ancient Vedic traditions from India, the soul enters the physical plane upon the baby's first breath and leaves with the last exhalation.

This was certainly how we experienced my father's death.

Psychology as Science

Psychology is defined as 'the scientific study of behavior and mental processes' and was first launched as an independent field of study by Wilhelm Wundt in 1879. Of course, people have been studying people, at least as far back as ancient Egypt. But Professor Wundt, a German physician, and philosopher, was the first person to call himself a psychologist and set up an experimental laboratory.

Up until then 'psychology' had merely been a branch of philosophy and for many years it retained those philosophical roots. Many of the great early contributions to our understandings of the human mind emerged more from thoughtful conclusions, based on careful observations of patients in treatment than the kind of double-blind lab experiments we're used to today. Great thinkers like Carl Jung, Sigmund Freud, and William James developed beautifully sophisticated maps and models for understanding the human mind and psyche.

I know that Freud has something of a bad name today – some of his theories seem pretty absurd and convoluted. And there's a reason for that. Freud's original investigations into 'hysteria' uncovered rampant incest and sexual molestation among the elite society of Vienna. Many of the men who happened to be his patrons were clearly molesting their own daughters or nieces! Needless to say, they weren't pleased with being outed.

Faced with a major crisis in his career, Freud caved, and the most ridiculous of his theories reflect that decision, essentially blaming the victims. Which is really a shame, beyond being a shameful thing to do, because much of Freud's other work was absolutely brilliant. This is the guy who discovered the subconscious mind!

Carl Jung, one of Freud's early colleagues, broke with him and developed his own models, exploring the collective unconscious, the shadow, the anima and animus, and archetypes. His work is highly regarded today and referred to as Depth or Transpersonal Psychology. I studied Jung in graduate school, and still find his concepts *very* helpful.

Alas, time marches on and things began to change for the study of the soul.

With the ascendancy of scientific materialism in the 20th century, psychology may have developed a bit of an inferiority complex. Philosophy was out. Experimental science was in. Pavlov's early work with salivating dogs set the stage for Behaviorism, which held that all human behavior was merely the result of conditioning. Children came into the world as a blank slate. Even as a callow 17-year-old college freshman, I knew *that* was bullshit.

I remember hearing my very first psychology professor explaining this 'blank slate' idea. He was a Behaviorist himself and quite a nervous fellow with a habit of giggling during his lectures. I wondered if he'd ever actually known or even encountered a baby. I found the idea laughable until I realized that blank slate or no, people *can* be conditioned and that there are powerful forces intent on doing so.

In my second year as a psych major at University of California San Diego, one of my textbooks was titled *The Prediction and Control of Human Behavior*. I'd always thought of psychology as the basis for counseling or therapy. UCSD seemed to have more corporate or governmental interests in mind. I found this extremely creepy and transferred to the University of Oregon, which had great Counseling and Humanistic Psychology departments.

Poor old psychology. Ashamed of its roots as mere philosophy it still tries so hard to be properly scientific. But how do you measure the Soul? Especially if you're keen on denying there actually is such a thing?

It's absurd to believe we can only know what's true if it's been 'scientifically' proven through lab experiments and double-blind studies. Especially since the vast majority of studies are done on either rats or college kids. Meaning no disrespect to college kids and rats, but are they seriously supposed to represent all of Humanity?

Scandals

And then there's the scandal of replication. Replication means the original experiment is repeated by another experimenter to see if they get the same results, and very few studies today are. There's no money in it. No prestige. But when 'important' studies actually *are* replicated, the results are usually *much* weaker or not even significant!

Experimental researchers are supposed to be objective observers; impartial Seekers of Truth. The expectations are strikingly similar to what we have for priests, who are supposed to take on the mantle of holiness by setting aside their worldly ambitions. And their sexuality. As we know, this hasn't always worked out so well!

Researchers are people. They have mortgages and car payments. Maybe they'd like to send their kids to good schools. They also have careers and often depend on grants and funding from corporate sponsors. University professors face tremendous pressure to publish – ideally something significant and *newsworthy.*

The double-blind format is supposed to safeguard against researcher bias. Apparently not so much. Here's a quote from Dr. Richard Horton, editor in chief of *The Lancet,* one of the most respected peer-reviewed medical journals:

> *The case against science is straightforward: much of the scientific literature, perhaps half, may simply be untrue. Afflicted by studies with small sample sizes, tiny effects, invalid exploratory analyses, and flagrant conflicts of interest, together with an obsession for pursuing fashionable trends of dubious importance, science has taken a turn towards darkness.*

This view is shared by Dr. Marcia Angell, physician and longtime Editor in Chief of the *New England Medical Journal* (NEMJ), another of the most prestigious peer-reviewed medical journals:

> *It is simply no longer possible to believe much of the clinical research that is published, or to rely on the judgment of trusted physicians or authoritative medical guidelines. I take no pleasure in this conclusion, which I reached slowly and reluctantly over my two decades as an editor of the New England Journal of Medicine*

If this is true of medical research, how much more so for psychological studies?

Don't get me wrong. I'm not anti-science. But science, or scientism, makes for a terrible religion. We should never have to take anything in science on faith, especially not the results of grant-funded institutional research studies. Especially when it comes to the study of the soul.

Your rational mind is impressive, but your heart and gut have their own wisdom. Just don't ask them *how* they reach their conclusions. They just do. It's foolish to ignore our 'gut feeling' about a person or situation. And does failing to 'follow our heart' ever turn out well?

Hacking Reality is, for the most part, based on old school psychology, metaphysics and esoteric sources of information – a pragmatic philosophical framework that I've found very useful in my work. I'm asking you to try these ideas on for size and be your own research study. I promise we won't need statistics to determine if the results are meaningful.

In the next chapter, we'll take a more in-depth look at the notion of Souls.

CHAPTER 5

You Are a Soul

Psychology is the study of the soul, but what exactly *is* the soul? I've got some interesting ideas about that I'd like to share with you. Ideas I've found useful in my own life and in my work with clients. There's really no way to prove if any of this material is true, and you certainly don't have to believe a word of it to benefit from *Hacking Reality*. Just for ease of communication though, I'll be presenting it all as established fact.

You don't have a Soul, you are a Soul. You have a body.

This quote is often misattributed to CS Lewis. It's a little unclear who actually said this, but I think they really nailed it.

You are a soul. Your life here on Earth has purpose and meaning. You actually volunteered to be here as part of the unfolding of Creation. You're here for education and entertainment and few, if any, events in your life have happened randomly. As discussed earlier, you mostly planned things out before you were born into a state of relative amnesia.

As Souls, we experience a great many lifetimes and grow and develop by going through them. I believe we're actually created in groups of around 1000 souls and most of the key players in our lives are likely from our group or *karass*, as author Kurt Vonnegut dubbed them. This is why some people seem instantly familiar to us. We've known them in and out of time.

Soul Ages

I've found the channeled teachings of Michael to be a fascinating and useful perspective on the human soul. According to Michael we start out our first lifetimes as 'Infant Souls,' focused mainly on survival issues. The material plane really takes some getting used to, much like our body does when we're first born. The amnesia of feeling cut off from the Divine is actually terrifying. Our sense of individuality as Infant Souls is rather undeveloped and we're often more identified with our tribe or family.

After gaining mastery of inhabiting a body and bumbling about in three dimensions, our next lifetimes are spent as 'Baby Souls'. The world is still pretty scary, but Baby Souls have discovered something that helps – The Rules! By carefully following social, political, and religious rules life feels a lot safer.

Fundamentalism is very popular with Baby Souls, who often become confused or angry with people who break The Rules or even question them. They're very keen on authority figures and easily confuse obedience and conformity with virtue. Unfortunately, they generally lack discernment and may be easily misled.

The ones misleading them are most likely 'Young Souls,' our next step up. As Young Souls, we've figured out that life is just a game and we want to win it, whether that means wealth, status, power, fame or some unholy combination thereof. Young Souls tend to be ambitious and driven, and breaking 'The Rules' is no problem at all if that's what it takes to win. Or better still - getting into a position to actually edit The Rules!

A classic example is a charismatic televangelist, promising everlasting salvation to his Baby Soul congregation. All they have to do is tithe their hard-earned dollars 'unto the Lord.' Or an ambitious state senator getting campaign donations by sponsoring legislation allowing toxic waste dumps near elementary schools.

With the possible exception of their closest friends and family, Young Souls don't realize yet that other people are actually real. Ethics are seen as an inside joke, arbitrary rules one can manipulate to control the masses and win the game. Young Souls are oblivious to the massive karma they're creating for themselves.

Happily, the ambition to leave one's mark on the world does have a wonderful upside. Many, perhaps most, of humanity's greatest achievements in art, literature, technology, architecture, and music came from Young Souls. Until very recently one had to actually *accomplish* something to be famous.

Eventually though, winning the game becomes meaningless. All of the prizes lose their luster as it slowly dawns on us that other people might actually be real and not just props in our own play. This is where the 'Mature Soul' level begins. It's a popular storyline for Hollywood – the hard-driving executive falls in love and loses his focus on money and success. He begins exploring emotions and meaning in a heartwarming tale of redemption.

Actually, this new awareness of others can come as quite a shock. One's *inner* world begins to come alive. The way Michael puts it: "It is a stirred-up, introspective time. There is more emotional centering here, more intensity, more schizophrenia, more pain, more suicide, more love, more sensuality, and probably more drugs to intensify it all than in any other period."

Needless to say, this engrossing drama can keep us busy for quite some time. Or lifetimes. Consider how many people become totally addicted to soap operas for years and years. Eventually though, as our empathy increases, other people start seeming less and less other. We get a handle on all the drama and passion, and realize at some point we've arrived in the 'Old Soul' camp.

Being an Old Soul means we've got a lot of lifetimes under our belt. We've built up a tremendous store of knowledge and wisdom based on countless experiences. Whether we have *access* to that wealth of experience is another matter and depends greatly on the personality we've chosen.

When we incarnate, we not only take on a body but also a personality. For those who've signed up for really difficult circumstances, the personality that develops through trauma can be incredibly tough to transcend. We're like Houdini escaping his straightjacket and chains while suspended upside down under water! Sometimes we don't quite make it.

For those of us who *do* achieve that deeper, wiser Old Soul perspective, it's usually not until our mid-30s, at the earliest. We've lived so many lifetimes and completed so many life lessons, but we've still got to deal with the challenges of *this* lifetime, and that can take some doing.

Ontogeny Recapitulates Phylogeny

In 1866 German naturalist Ernst Haeckel coined this term, *'ontogeny recapitulates phylogeny'* which proposes that during our development in the womb, we go through all the stages of evolution – fish to reptile to simple mammal to human. Modern biology isn't really keen on Haeckel's notion, but it applies pretty well to soul ages.

Infants are easily freaked out. Two-year-olds are learning the rules and stamp their foot, screaming, "It's not fair!" Nine-year-olds want to be popular, win at games, get an A on the test. Teens get crushes, go steady, get their hearts broken and start to ask the big questions, "Who am I, and why are we here?"

We really only go as far as our Soul has already progressed, then the life lessons really kick in. A Young Soul, for example, will view relationships through the lens of winning the game. He'll want to date the most popular girl in school and likely marry for money, connections or status. He might seek out 'arm candy' or a 'trophy wife' in hopes of impressing others. He literally doesn't know what he's missing. Not until he's nearing graduation to Mature Soul.

Old Souls

Speaking of status, being an Old Soul doesn't make one superior to younger souls. A first grader might be *way* smarter than any of the eighth graders. Everyone grows up and graduates eventually.

That said, Old Souls often do have a lot to share and often have easy access to a variety of amazing skills, sometimes to the level of mastery. Ironically though, they can also demonstrate an almost total lack of worldly ambition. This detachment can really frustrate and perplex their younger Soul students and admirers!

Old Souls are generally here to wrap things up, completing old karma and unfinished business. They might be exploring intellectual, philosophical and spiritual issues or projects that don't even register for younger souls. There's often a strong aversion to anything which might create new karmic entanglements.

Old Souls are often great teachers, though perhaps with few students. Their lack of personal ambition and desire to live a quiet life keeps them modest. They're sometimes plagued by loneliness, self-deprecation, and depression. Loneliness because it's hard to relate to the passions and struggles of younger souls. Self-deprecation because their ambitions are turned inward toward self-perfection. Depression because awareness of life beyond death can make Earthly life seem drab and harsh by comparison. Fortunately, these are all issues that can be addressed with EFT tapping.

One of the final tests to graduate and transcend Earthly life is to become genuinely fond of being here.

Empathy

Soul age has a great deal to do with how you experience reality. The older your soul, the more able you are to experience other people, and other beings, as real unto themselves and not just props in your own play. This is an awakening from the perception of isolation into a community of fellow travelers and allies.

We really start feeling this as Mature Souls, or as Old Souls going through that period of our life. Other people are not only real; they're the most fascinating thing ever!

Mature Souls will still hurt other people, but out of passion rather than callous disregard. At this stage, our dogs and cats become real to us. We see their personalities and understand them as actual persons. And with this awareness, comes respect and empathy.

Old Souls have the capacity to experience *everything* as alive and real. Not just other people. Not just animals. Even the plant kingdom becomes populated with beings, newly perceived. Ancient redwood trees and potted philodendrons alike become peers in consciousness and potential allies. The same is true for the mineral kingdom.

I've known people who were *way* into crystals and gemstones. I'll admit I may have thought them just a little bit kooky in the past. Maybe some of them really were a bit kooky, but I realize now they were tuned into something real that I hadn't perceived yet.

Spirit Guides

I believe that you are never truly alone and never have been, even for an instant. Remember Vonnegut's notion of our *karass*? We have a lot of teammates, and not all of them are incarnate at any given time. I promise that at least a few of them agreed to be 'spirit guides' for you. These are old friends, who watch over you from the astral plane, cheering you on.

How much you want to be aware of them, and whether you want their help and guidance is entirely up to you. Accomplishing something all by ourselves can be very satisfying. On the other hand, having a support crew can be pretty amazing.

It's okay to ask your spirit guides for help and guidance. And asking is pretty much required. Without that invitation, any help from them would be interference, a violation of your free will and sovereignty.

So if you want help, make sure and ask. My own guides show up for me as the quiet voice of intuition. Whenever I'm about to do something especially stupid, they're liable to point out other options. And when I work with clients, they quietly provide insight, information and helpful suggestions. So quietly, I'm tempted to take all the credit! But really, I figure they're probably chatting up my client's spirit guides. It's basically a team effort.

By the way, spirit guides are not Angels. They're just old friends who happen to be between lifetimes. Angels are something else entirely. I don't really know a lot about them, but I'm pretty sure they're for real. And it's the same deal where if you want their help, you have to ask.

Okay, now we've covered the *really* weird woo-woo stuff. If that was a big stretch for you, relax, take a nice deep breath. In the next few chapters we're going to move on to more solid ground, namely Newtonian Classical Mechanics and then the extremely solid Materialist view of reality. No angel, devas, spirit guides or souls allowed!

CHAPTER 6

Playing by the Rules – From a Clockwork Universe to Quantum Reality

In September 2015 I got busted by a monk in Westminster Abbey. He was wearing a green polyester robe and had one of those coiled wire earbuds like Agent Smith from *The Matrix*.

Westminster Abbey is an amazing place and has an equally amazing number of NO PHOTOGRAPHY signs posted. I'm a pretty keen photographer, but no scofflaw. I was doing fine until we hit Sir Isaac Newton's tomb. It's pretty impressive, with his reclining figure in marble attended by two little cherubs. I guess something in me just snapped.

My camera was hanging around my neck and ever so slowly, ever so discreetly, I switched it on and without even really aiming I pressed the shutter a few times. And was promptly busted by this medieval Agent Smith who very politely suggested I put the lens cap on. I thought for sure I'd end up in prison, but he didn't even throw me out!

I paid for my crime by feeling very guilty. But I still have the pictures.

Sir Isaac Newton has always been a hero of mine. That's my excuse. His scientific and mathematical contributions were astonishing. And liberating. Newton gifted us the Laws of Nature and look at all the cool stuff we've done based on his discoveries.

Another of my great heroes, Rupert Sheldrake, is still alive and much easier to photograph. He once graciously allowed me to take a selfie with him. Like Newton, Sheldrake is an Englishman, a Cambridge fellow and a pioneering scientist. Whereas Newton explored physics (and alchemy) at Cambridge, Sheldrake is primarily a biologist.

Mr. Sheldrake suggests that the 'Laws of Nature' may actually be more like customs or habits than laws. He points out that the very idea of 'laws' is rather anthropomorphic. Humans invented laws and only recently at that. Historically, most human societies were organized around customs which developed more or less organically over very long periods of time.

Customs are better able to adapt to changing circumstances, whereas laws are a bit more set in stone. Or literally *chiseled* into stone if you go all the way back to the Code of Hammurabi.

No Free Lunch

In high school physics class, we were taught Newton's First Law of Thermodynamics, which states that energy (in a closed system) cannot be created or destroyed. That's why 'free energy machines' are always regarded as fake and the inventors who designed them frauds. Every so often one of these devices will show up on a local TV program. Experts are brought forward to heap derision and contempt on the inventor. No matter how convincing one of these devices seems to be or how sincere the promoter, it *has* to be a hoax because it violates one of the primary Laws of Physics.

This is such a shame. Free energy machines would come in *really* handy right about now. Damn that First Law of Thermodynamics.

Well, guess what? It turns out Isaac Newton just made this one up. Seriously. As a good Christian, Newton accepted church doctrine that God created the Universe "In the beginning." Newton envisioned God as the Great Clockmaker in the Sky, creating it as a perfect, complete system and then setting it into motion. Just like a clock.

It just made sense that everything was there, all matter and all energy, "In the beginning." That's why this was the First Law.

Except this isn't actually true. Astrophysicists tell us there's nowhere *near* enough matter or energy to account for their observations. To make their equations work out they've come up with something called 'dark energy' and 'dark matter.' The matter and energy Newton described seems to be less than 5 percent of the total!

And no one knows what the hell the 'dark' stuff is or how it behaves. What we *do* know is that Newton simply made up the First Law of Thermodynamics as an article of religious faith. So, can we have our free energy machines now? Please?

The Mechanics of Reality

Newton's laws of nature are known as Classical Mechanics – "the set of physical laws describing the motion of bodies under the influence of a system of forces." They answered most of our big questions about how the world worked and paved the way for handy things like the Industrial Revolution.

But they didn't answer quite *all* of our questions, and about 100 years ago another bright fellow by the name of Albert Einstein showed up to give us the Theory of General Relativity and to rather reluctantly set the stage for Quantum Mechanics.

Newtonian Classical Mechanics describes normal reality – the stuff that's readily observable. It gave us cool things like steam locomotives and jet engines. Quantum Mechanics, on the other hand, is freaking weird. It gave us lasers, computers and cell phones, but generally defies common sense and seems to happen only on the teensiest tiny microscopic level. A hundred years later it still hasn't really caught on with the public.

These are not *Competing Narratives*. It's just that the reality that Newton's Classical Mechanics describes so well is merely a subset of the greater reality. Of course, this just happens to be the subset of reality we call home, but it's *not* the most fundamental level of reality. Not even close.

Watching a movie up on the big screen, we don't usually realize what we're seeing is actually light shining through a lot of still frame photographs, one after the other. The projector makes this happen so fast that our minds can conveniently put all of those still frames together into one long moving picture. It seems very real to us, but it's actually an illusion.

In much the same way, those billiard balls whose motion Newton described so well certainly seem real. We can pick them up and feel their weight. If we hit one with the pool cue, it'll pretty much go in the direction we expect and make a satisfying clack when it hits the other balls. (Unless I'm playing. I pretty much suck at pool).

But those billiard balls are made of wood, which is made from cellulose, which is composed of molecules, which are strings of atoms, which are made of subatomic particles, which are actually pure energy winking in and out of existence from space. When the billiard balls clack together, nothing is actually touching because there's no *thing* actually there – it's all energy. The clacking sound is made by a discharge of energy when the electrons get close enough together. Einstein once wrote:

> *The deeper we delve into the atomic world, the more we see that there is no solid, there are only relationships between energies. All matter is merely energy condensed to a slow vibration, everything you think of as the material world dissolves on the sub atomic levels. Literally reality is an illusion, albeit a very persistent illusion.*

You know all of this stuff, right? But it's hard to keep it in mind when we're walking around in our bodies. And speaking of bodies, they're made out of energy too. Which is really good news for us when we get around to hacking the reality of our physical problems.

Unfortunately, not everyone is down with this energetic reality stuff. Before we go any further, let's tackle the anti-miracle mindset of Materialism. It may even now be plaguing you like an itchy wet blanket, stifling the growing excitement I'm hoping to engender here.

CHAPTER 7

The Myth of Materialism

Materialists believe that matter is the only reality. Anything that can't be perceived with our senses or measured with scientific instruments is unreal and unworthy of consideration. Consciousness is considered an 'epiphenomenon of brain activity that has no real significance. It can't be measured so it shouldn't be studied.

This is an astonishing idea, given that consciousness is required to entertain the idea of Materialism in the first place.

This worldview holds that since identity and consciousness are generated by the brain, once the body dies and brain activity stops, they simply cease to exist. There can be no life beyond the physical body and any interest in exploring the issue is met with severe contempt. Materialists are often fervent atheists and have made something of a religion out of their version of science, replacing the priest's cassock for the researcher's lab coat and clipboard.

Because matter is all that is real, and human consciousness is accidental, and of no real importance, life itself is inherently meaningless. There is no purpose to existence, beyond the biological imperatives to survive and procreate. We are skin-encapsulated egos, isolated from nature and one another. Our identity is extinguished after a brief, meaningless existence prone to the suffering caused by random events.

What a grim, dysfunctional worldview! Since nothing is sacred, nature is simply a storage bank of raw materials waiting to be harvested and human beings are of no more consequence than any other beast – ripe for exploitation by their masters. Perhaps this is why it has held sway for so long in the institutions of higher learning, it certainly serves the interests of the bankers and corporations.

Most people who've been indoctrinated into Materialism aren't quite so extreme, and yet it puts a serious damper on their reality. Ironically, the science behind Materialism is severely antiquated. Perhaps behind the knee jerk anger, contempt and general abhorrence Materialists display towards all things 'woo woo' there's some insecurity.

If you've been swayed by this world view, allow me to give you a gentle kick in the ass here and there throughout this book. Science and dogma are a very bad combination, so let's get it out of your (operating) system.

Superstition

In psychology, the word *superstition* refers to an invalid cause and effect belief, where a random coincidence is ascribed meaning. Let's say I'm a pigeon and food pellets are delivered to me at random, one day a pellet comes when I happen to pick my foot up. If by chance this happens again, I may develop a belief that picking my foot up will cause the food pellet to appear. Pretty soon I may start dancing whenever I get hungry.

Human beings seem even more prone to this sort of thing than pigeons. We're very good at noticing coincidences and seem hardwired to ascribe meaning to them. Some people believe in omens and may feel that God, or the gods, or nature, or spirits of their ancestors are trying to tell them something in a symbolic language of events.

From the rational perspective of a Materialist, this is just contemptible superstitious rubbish. There are no gods, no angels, no spirits of anyone's ancestors, and nature is just an organized collection of raw materials. It's utter nonsense to believe otherwise and totally unscientific.

Interestingly, Sir Isaac Newton himself believed in God and spent much of his life exploring alchemy. Rupert Sheldrake makes the interesting point that the word *Matter* comes from the Latin for 'mother.' In rejecting the Sky Father image of God, they unwittingly embraced the Earth Mother instead. Not that this has done *her* a lot of good!

Materialism was initially a rather insignificant fringe philosophy, but then came the French and Bolshevik revolutions. In both cases an extremely corrupt Church was joined at the hip with the aristocracy, justifying the appalling conditions of the peasants as 'divinely ordered.' Revolutionaries seized upon atheism as a way of breaking the influence of the Church, and the seemingly scientific views of Materialism that seemed to give atheism credence.

Materialism also helped support the Industrial Revolution. No other philosophy so aptly justifies treating essential living ecosystems as mere collections of dead raw materials ripe for the taking. Or human workers as expendable, exploitable losers in the inevitable economic fight for the survival of the fittest.

As you can probably tell, I'm not a big fan of the Materialist world view, which ultimately tells us our lives are meaningless, and our deepest desires and longings for love and self-expression are utterly insignificant. It's a fantastic backdrop for a dystopian horror film, but not much good for our hacking purposes.

The fact that it's really just scientifically outmoded metaphysics is good news for those of us who'd like to transform our lives gracefully and in a timely manner.

Synchronicity

Carl Jung coined the term 'synchronicity' to shine a light on meaningful coincidences we can't rationally explain. He described it as an "acausal connecting principle," suggesting that events could be connected not just by causation, but also by *meaning*. Could meaning be related to entanglement?

The word coincidence literally means more than one incident happening at the same time – that's a *co-incidence*. These days people use the word to imply the events are *not* connected in any meaningful way. They just happened to happen at the same time with no clear, obvious, logical connection

If I flip a light switch and the light comes on, no one is likely to say, "Whoa, what a coincidence!" Even though most of us probably have no clear idea of how electricity actually works, there's still an obvious causal relationship. It works every time.

But if I happen to sneeze and 2 seconds later a bird hits the living room window, most people would ascribe no meaning there. The two events *do* take place together at the same time but were *just* a coincidence. And it's very unlikely to ever happen again.

But what if you just happened to be thinking about your old college roommate, Sarah? You haven't thought of her in years, but later that day your sister asks, "Hey, remember Sarah? Whatever happened to her?" Or perhaps her picture just happens to be tagged in a photo that pops up on Facebook. What a weird coincidence, huh?

Random Chance

Most educated people have been subtly indoctrinated in the Materialist world view, and part of this is a belief in *randomness*. The idea that things just happen randomly by chance is such a strong conceptual bias that it's generally taken for granted.

I'd like to suggest that our belief in randomness is in fact just a belief. There's no way to prove it, so really it's just an article of faith. And do we believe in randomness because it seems true? Or does it seem true because we believe in it?

If you really think about it, what *is* randomness? How does it work? Is it some eternal principle that's always true everywhere? If matter is supposed to be the only real thing, then where and how does randomness operate? One might ask, where does it live?

Why is this relevant? The notion of randomness is closely related to the belief that life is meaningless. If things just happen randomly, by definition, there's no meaning behind them. Shit happens, and there's no rhyme or reason to it. There's no real purpose to anything. We evolved to eat and procreate, and that's the end of it. Any notion of living a virtuous life is just delusional. Whoever dies with the most toys is the winner.

My point here is that Materialism in general, and randomness in particular, are metaphysical belief systems, all gussied up to look scientific. They've been given a veneer of sophistication, but there's no scientific proof that life is random or meaningless. To the contrary, there's some delightful evidence that it's not. Consider this wonderful experiment by French researcher, René Peoc'h in 1995.

Love vs. Random Chance

René Peoc'h designed a simple robot to move about the smooth floor of a room. It was something like a Roomba, whose motions were directed by a random number generator. Placing a light atop the robot and a camera on the ceiling, Peoc'h was able to graphically track its path over time. As random chance would have it, in its own jerky way, the robot eventually covered most of the floor.

Mr. Peoc'h then took a group of 15 baby chicks and imprinted them with the robot. Chicks are apt to imprint on whatever moving object they first encounter, which then becomes Mama. Once they were imprinted with the robot, he put the chicks in a small transparent cage at one end of the room, where they could easily see their robot mom moving around.

The results were astonishing. The robot stayed two and a half times more on the side of the room where the chicks were. This was repeated with 80 groups of chicks, and the results were consistent. This should *not* have happened! The robot's movements were entirely controlled by the random number generator, so somehow the chicks were able to influence random chance.

Interestingly, Peoc'h tried the same experiment with baby rabbits, but they were initially frightened by the robot, which then responded somehow by mostly staying on the other side of the room! After a few weeks though, when the baby rabbits got used to it, the robot began spending most of its time near them.

If baby chicks and rabbits can override a default setting like randomness, what might you and I be able to pull off? Of course, it might be easier for them, being free from indoctrination by conventional Western education.

Quantum mechanics has proven again and again that our observations influence physical reality. And our beliefs, expectations, and intentions totally influence our observations. I invite you to examine, and possibly suspend, your own beliefs around random chance.

Opening up to the idea of meaningful coincidences is one step closer to accepting and expecting miracles. Einstein famously said:

> *There are only two ways to live your life. One is as though nothing is a miracle. The other is as though everything is a miracle.*

Are Good and Evil Found in Nature?

People generally assume that morality is a purely human creation. In fact, the idea of "Nature red in tooth and claw" has been pushed relentlessly for a very long time. We've been led to believe that selfishness is natural. The implication being that altruistic, moral or virtuous behavior is artificial, unnatural and ultimately misguided.

But is this really true? Natural systems are balanced on a continuum of evolution versus entropy. An evolving system becomes ever more complex, with the various plant, animal, mineral and water participants increasingly interdependent and entwined. This sort of complexity gives the overall system increased resiliency. The guiding principle here is symbiosis.

The opposite end of the continuum is entropy – the collapse and disintegration of a complex system into its component parts. The system becomes degraded and increasingly fragile. A key driver here is often parasitism, which means one of the participants extracts energy from the system without providing any benefit in return.

This is not the same as a predator/prey relationship. Predators generally *benefit* the community of their prey. Culling the weaker members enhances the strength of the herd, for example. By contrast, parasitical relationships are actually pathological – fleas, ticks, and mosquitoes not only weaken their hosts, they may even introduce disease pathogens that ultimately destroy them.

Is it possible that our cultural ideas of good vs. evil developed from observing natural systems over millennia? Symbiotic altruism vs. parasitical selfishness. Flourishing diversity and health versus barrenness, death, and disease.

I believe Materialism has been enshrined in our halls of learning not because it offers the most accurate or 'scientific' model, but rather because it supports and justifies parasitical behavior. Materialism as a worldview strikes me as ultimately evil, in the sense that it's entropic and anti-life.

At the time of this writing, vertically integrated hyper-parasitical corporate structures have become so powerful and so efficient at extracting energy, wealth and value from every system they interact with, it's no exaggeration to say that life on Earth is being actively threatened.

The good news is that changing your *own* life and stepping into your own power actually benefits everyone. Taking time to focus on your own personal evolution is not a selfish act at all. We're all connected – entangled in a holographic expanding Universe. Hacking your own reality is a gift that keeps on giving.

Imagine finding yourself in a hot air balloon that's about to crash into the treetops. You need more loft! More elevation! Quick, better find some sandbags to dump overboard.

On our expedition to a better Alternate Universe, sandbag #1 is labeled *Western Materialist Worldview*. Tossing that one over the side can be very enlightening.

In the next chapter, we'll take a look at some of the strange ways quantum reality differs from our normal experience of the world. And, because that's a deeper, more 'real' level of reality, perhaps we can leverage some of those differences to pull off a miracle or two.

CHAPTER 8

Leveraging Quantum Weirdness

L et's take a look at some of the stranger aspects of quantum reality and how they might help us bend the conventional rules for what's possible.

Blueprints in the Field

If your body really is made out of energy, winking in and out of space in every moment, then how does it know how to maintain its shape? How do all of your trillions of cells know how to work together to make your body a living organism? What organizes the organism?

For that matter, how does the stapler on my desk just happen to be materializing there? What tells the energy how to materialize, so things stay relatively consistent for us? These are very helpful questions for our hacking purposes!

Everything that manifests in our physical plane of reality has a pattern, or what I like to call a blueprint. In quantum physics there's the concept of the Matrix – the underlying Field from which everything that exists or has existed or will exist emerges. This is also called the 'quantum field'.

The blueprint for your body is a subfield within the quantum field, much like a wave in the ocean. Each wave has its own essence or being, as does every drop of water within that wave. And the wave and drops of water are inseparable from the entirety of the ocean. In much the same way, the field that organizes your pancreas or eyelashes is part of the overall field for your entire body.

This can be a very helpful mindset when there's a physical problem with our body. Or really any physical problem we encounter.

Isolation by Design

Even if you accept the idea that your body is made of energy appearing out of space and connected through the Matrix with everything else in the Universe, unless you're tripping on psychedelics, that's probably not your immediate experience.

Thanks to the way our bodies and senses are set up, we tend to experience ourselves as physically distinct from others. We live within the boundaries of our skin, experiencing ourselves as individuals. We may be able to connect with others emotionally or intellectually, but physically we're on our own.

The obvious downside here is *feeling* alone, cut off from everybody and everything else. The default nature of our self-awareness can make us pretty lonesome.

The good news is that our isolation is mere illusion. Your consciousness is temporarily inhabiting your body which is manifesting as an indivisible part of the Matrix, along with everyone and everything else – one wave in the endless ocean of the Universe.

The concept of quantum entanglement, which Einstein called "spooky action at a distance," suggests our connection with all of life. This is truly the deepest level of reality. So all those bumper stickers are right – we really are all one.

That said, some connections are stronger than others. We seem to have a much stronger connection with those we know and really care about. That just makes sense, right?

Rupert Sheldrake has done massive studies on what he calls 'telephone telepathy.' Back in the days before caller ID, when the phone rang you never knew who was calling. Except that people often *did* know. Even if the call was totally unexpected.

Sheldrake found that this is actually a very common experience. Some would call it *paranormal,* but it's actually just plain normal. Perhaps you've experienced it yourself? I certainly have.

Years ago, I picked up the phone to call my friend Meredith, and there was no dial tone. Instead, I could hear breathing! It was Meredith! I heard her say to her husband, "Steve, something's wrong with the phone, it isn't ringing." I picked up the instant she'd finished dialing my number. That was spooky!

Because we *are* so connected, the possibilities and potential for remote or surrogate healing work are vast. I'll be sharing some practical techniques in a later chapter.

The Power of Now

About a month before his death in 1955, Albert Einstein wrote:

> *People like us, who believe in physics, know that the distinction between past, present, and future is only a stubbornly persistent illusion.*

It seems that within quantum mechanics there's really no accounting for linear time. I can't pretend to understand the mathematics of it, but it seems that everything is happening *now*. Eckhart Tolle was really on to something.

Einstein called time a persistent illusion, but the word persuasive also comes to mind. Our entire biological existence seems pretty darn linear. Cradle to grave. That's about as real as it gets, from our point of view.

But again, the movie you see up on the big screen isn't a moving picture. It's a whole lot of single pictures. Still frames. One after the other. Stop the film, and you can examine each one of them.

I believe that in the movie of our life, the still frames are actually Moments. Each moment is it's own 'now'. Each now exists forever in the quantum field. The movie of our life only seems real when its run through the 'remembering' projector and that projector only seems to run in one direction. And that's our experience of time.

Remembering the 'past' is easy and automatic, but very few of us ever remember the 'future'. It does happen though. It's called precognition – a well-documented phenomenon. Perhaps déjà vu is precognition on a smaller, more immediate scale?

If every moment of our life is happening now, does that mean we can access any or all of them? The answer is Yes! Even those moments we can't consciously remember are stored and available.

Retrocausation

Imagine languishing in the hospital with serious, potentially life-threatening blood poisoning. Would you want someone praying for you? Even a total stranger? I hope your answer is yes.

In the year 2000, a research study was carefully designed to examine the possible effects of 'intercessory prayer; – prayer on behalf of someone else. The prayers were done remotely for hospital patients suffering from sepsis, a bloodstream infection. Dr. Leonard Leibovici took the records of 3393 patients and used a random number generator to assign them to either a control group or an intervention group which received prayer for 'well-being and full recovery.'

Dr. Leibovici chose for the study three measurable, objective outcomes: mortality, length of stay in hospital and duration of fever. For the first measure, there was no significant change in the death rate between the two groups. I guess if your number is up, that's that.

But in the other two measures, there *was* a significant improvement. The group that received prayers spent much less time in the hospital, and their fevers broke much sooner.

Outcomes like this are not uncommon in studies of prayer. To ensure maximum credibility, Dr. Leibovici set up his experiment very carefully to prevent bias – neither the hospital staff nor the patients themselves knew who was getting prayed for. In fact, they didn't know anyone was getting prayed for or that a study was even being carried out!

What makes this particular study so interesting, and dare I say mind-blowing, is that the prayer was *retroactive*. The study was done in the year 2000, but Dr. Leibovici chose records of patients who had been treated from 1990 to 1996 – 4 to 10 years earlier! Let that sink in.

In other words, someone prayed for patients who had been sick years earlier. They'd already died or gotten better and been discharged four to ten years before any praying was done, and this was not disclosed to those who were praying. But clearly, the group that was prayed for fared much better than the control group. The prayer not only worked, it somehow worked backwards in time. This is an example of a phenomenon called retrocausation.

One summer I got to work in a movie theater. The films would come to us in big, flat, round metal cans. The whole movie was in there – hundreds of thousands of still frames on the reel in sequence. The beginning, middle, and end of the movie were all there at the same time. And though it goes by incredibly fast, only one still frame at a time is illuminated by the projector.

In quantum reality, our lifetimes are 'in the can' apparently – all the moments present in the eternal now. Today we have ways of accessing these moments directly, and they can be *edited*. Rather than praying for 'intercession' we can intervene ourselves directly, retroactively. This then *changes* the movie from that moment forward.

In other words, going back and revising moments from your past can literally change your present reality – retrocausation. This is the basis for Matrix Reimprinting, which I described in the first chapter. It's a key aspect of hacking reality because *some* of those moments hold the key to massive transformation.

Schrödinger's Pizza

The Double Slit Experiment is the most replicated experiment in the history of science. It's also considered the most elegant and beautiful. Researchers were trying to figure out whether electrons act as a particle or a wave, which is kind of a big deal, as far as understanding physical reality.

It turns out they can act like either, which was unexpected. But weirder still, whether they act like a wave or a particle depends on whether we're looking or not!

The implication seems to be that there is no objective reality. The smallest particles making up physical reality actually change what they're doing depending on whether someone is watching or not. In other words, the observer changes the observed by observing.

This ties into the principle of *Superposition* which suggests that all possible states that can exist, do exist *until* an observation occurs. To put it a different way, as you go through your day your observations are continually collapsing probability wavefronts. Your consciousness is imbued with reality creating powers.

Schrödinger's Cat is a famous thought experiment in which a cat is sealed in a box along with a vial of cyanide gas, poised to be released if a random number generator produces a pre-selected number. Superposition theory suggests the cat is both alive and dead until you open the box.

Ironically, Schrödinger was trying to demonstrate that quantum effects don't translate to our macro world. He assumed the idea of a cat being both alive *and* dead was so obviously and impossibly ludicrous that people would abandon the idea of quantum effects occurring in our own world. A total fail for Schrödinger!

Turns out most people have no real problem conceiving of this kitty cat paradox. Perhaps because cats have nine lives anyway?

Just for fun (and borrowing ideas from physicist Cynthia Sue Larson and *The Onion*), let's replace the cat with a pizza.

Imagine you've ordered a veggie pizza over the phone. Unbeknownst to you, everyone involved with that pizza – the guy who took your order, the guy who made it and even the delivery boy were all totally stoned off their butts.

When the delivery boy finally shows up (about an hour late) he's not really sure which pizza was yours, but hands you one anyway. Since the pizza parlor only makes two kinds of pizza though, he's totally certain it's either veggie or pepperoni. For sure. And for you, as a vegetarian, the stakes are high!

According to superposition that pizza is *both* veggie and pepperoni *until* you open the box and take a look. Your observation collapses the wavefront and all those subatomic particles coalesce into greasy orange pepperoni *or* mushrooms and green bell pepper slices. It's one or the other. Good luck!

So here it is in a nutshell: Our observations collapse probability wave fronts that coalesce into our reality. And our observations are influenced by our expectations, which in turn develop from our beliefs, including incorrect, limiting beliefs resulting from decisions made during traumatic experiences. Thanks to the reality of quantum time we can return to those traumas and edit them, which, thanks to the nature of superposition, generates retrocausation effects in your life.

I realize I haven't covered all aspects of that last paragraph yet, but thanks to the nature of books, all the information is already in your hands. Just keep reading.

In the next chapter, we'll go even deeper down the Quantum Mechanics rabbit hole, taking a look at multiple universes and how we're already moving back and forth between them. And how we might do so on purpose.

CHAPTER 9

Stepping into Parallel Universes

Thanks to countless sci-fi movies and books, the concept of multiple universes is widely familiar. Could it really be true? Are there multiple universes existing side by side, similar but different in key ways? While it's not a settled matter among physicists, I'll go out on a limb and say yes, almost certainly.

Imagine a ream of paper standing on one edge, 500 sheets stacked together, each one touching the sheets on either side and yet each being its own individual paper, parallel to all the others. There's really not much space between those sheets of paper.

Let's say that your Universe is one of those sheets of paper. The sheets on either side are incredibly similar, and yet some small thing is different. Perhaps that difference is something very trivial. But if you were to travel sideways across the ream, the further from your own sheet you go, the greater the differences would be.

I suspect we're shifting between very similar Universes, the sheets closest to us if you will, on a pretty regular basis. We don't usually notice because a) we don't even know this can happen, b) the differences are too small to really register, *or* c) as we shift into new realities our memories shift as well.

Except sometimes they don't.

About ten years ago I was talking with a friend who happened to mention blue whales. I said, "Isn't it a shame they were driven to extinction?" My friend was taken aback and said, "What are you talking about? Blue whales aren't extinct. They're swimming around in the ocean right now! You can see them on YouTube."

Well, that was really great news, but also a total surprise. I clearly remember being told in 3rd grade that they were extinct. A conventional explanation would be that either I simply misunderstood my teacher, or that she herself was mistaken and gave our class false information.

Maybe, but I don't think so. For 40 years no one had ever mentioned blue whales to me. I *love* whales. I've gone out whale watching. I've seen documentaries on whales. My guess is that somehow I made a lateral transfer into a different *and better* Universe that still has blue whales. And for whatever reason, my memory didn't automatically change when that happened.

The Mandela Effect

In recent years this sort of thing seems to be happening with large segments of the population. It's been called the Mandela Effect after Nelson Mandela, the anti-apartheid activist who went on to become South Africa's president. When Nelson Mandela died on December 5, 2013, a great many people were astonished. They thought he'd died in prison back in the 1980s. They were *certain* of it, and many claimed to have seen his funeral procession.

A rational explanation might be that they'd simply confused Mandela with another activist, Steve Biko, who actually did die in police custody in September 1977. Easy to get these black activists confused, right? Wrong! People are adamant about their memories, and there were so many of them; it became a phenomenon.

There are a great many examples of the Mandela Effect today, most of them rather trivial, involving pop culture. Just for fun, here are a few for your own memory test. Please note your answers, and don't cheat by looking ahead!

1. Darth Vader says "_____, I am your father."
2. "_____ _____ on the wall, who is the fairest of them all?"
3. Is the TV show called "Sex in the City" or "Sex and the City"?

4. From the Bible "The ____ lies down with the lamb."

5. The Beatles sing "What would you ____ if I sang out of tune, would you stand up and walk out on me..."

6. Mr. Rogers sings "It's a beautiful day in ____ neighborhood."

7. Forrest Gump says "Life ____ like a box of chocolates."

8. Are the cartoons called "Loony Tunes" or "Loony Toons"?

9. In the US, Thanksgiving is on the _____ Thursday in November.

10. The final lyrics in the Queen song We Are the Champions: "...no time for losers, 'cause we are the champions _____."

11. C3PO, the android from Star Wars was all gold – True or False?

12. How many states does the United States have?

13. The color "chartreuse" is a shade of _____.

See end of the chapter for the 'correct' answers

Depending on your age, some of the 'correct' answers may surprise you. In fact, you'll likely think my 'correct' answers are totally bogus. If you try to prove/confirm your memory though, you just might be disappointed, or even shocked. Old photos, textbooks, record albums or movie clips seem to have changed! That's where this starts to get *really* weird.

Again, the conventional explanation is that you're simply remembering wrong (along with a sizable percentage of the population.) A less popular explanation is that you've shifted into a slightly alternate parallel Universe, but without the corresponding change in memory.

I first encountered the Mandela Effect idea at a lecture by physicist Cynthia Sue Larson. As I recall, some of the audience members became rather upset by the changes she was pointing out. One change I found hard to accept was about the placement of the kidneys. Where do you think they are?

In massage school, I remember being taught that the kidneys were right above the pelvis and below the rib cage on the back side of the body. It was important to know since we weren't supposed to put a lot of pressure on them.

Dr. Larson showed us a number of images placing them much higher – up in the lower rib cage! Some of those images were from old medical textbooks! I was astonished. Checking Google just now shows images featuring both placements, which are markedly different. Perhaps I'm on the borderline between Universes.

Many of us have a very strong preference for reality staying put. We don't want our kidneys moving around, or even familiar pop culture references changing on us.

Stability is ideal if you have a nice cozy reality where everything is working out pretty well. On the other hand, if your personal life is stuck and frustrating, if Nature is on the ropes, and society as a whole seems to be sliding sideways into a dystopian nightmare, then this whole idea of shifting realities becomes a lot more intriguing.

The question comes up – if we really are making lateral transfers in and out of nearby parallel Universes, can we do so intentionally? And rather than weird, random and inconsequential changes, can we traverse in a significantly positive direction, on purpose?

Yes, we can. That's what Hacking Reality is really all about.

But what is it, exactly, that does this traversing? What makes you, *YOU*, whichever Universe you happen to be passing through? We'll explore this further in a discussion of morphic fields.

Here are the 'correct' answers. Though some of them seem to shift and change fairly often!

1. In our current time stream Darth Vader says "No, I am your father."
2. It's "magic mirror on the wall."
3. Currently, it's 'Sex *and* the City'
4. Apparently, it's 'The wolf lies down with the lamb'....!
5. "What would you *think* if I sang out of tune..." I think that's wrong!
6. 'It's a beautiful day in *this* neighborhood.'
7. 'Life *was* a box of chocolates.'
8. It's Tunes. At least now it is.
9. Fourth! I distinctly remember it as the Third. Here's a quote I found from a Mandela Effect website:

My husband's birthday is Nov. 23. We have been married 11 years. We've always celebrated his birthday during Thanksgiving while family is together. Multiple times his birthday has fallen on Thanksgiving Day. Because of the proximity of his birthday and the holiday, I feel that it's unlikely I'm remembering that wrong. When I asked him what day Thanksgiving is, he responded without a moment's hesitation that it's on the 3rd Thursday in November. I was almost physically ill when I googled the question and saw that it's been the "4th Thursday in November since the time of Abraham Lincoln's presidency.

10. The end is now ".....cause we are the champions." No more "...of the world." My daughter played the song for me, and we were both shocked – it had changed!

11. False. He now has one *silver* leg! It's quite distinct in the pictures I'm seeing.

12. 50. Duh! But *many* people are certain it's either 51 or 52.

13. Green. Weirdly enough, many people remember it as a kind of reddish purple.

CHAPTER 10

Morphic Fields

When I was a little boy I loved playing with magnets. It was so weird how they would stick to some things and not others, or how they would push another magnet away with some unseen force.

Unseen forces have not always been popular. Imagine playing a radio, or using a flashlight in the 1600s. You'd likely be burned at the stake for doing the work of the Devil.

We may be a bit more sophisticated today. Most of us have only a very dim idea of why the overhead light comes on when we flip the switch, or how our smartphone works, we don't consider this supernatural. These things are well understood by modern science and just part of everyday life. No one doubts the existence of magnetic, electromagnetic and gravitational fields.

Do you suppose there might be *other* field systems we still haven't discovered yet? Field systems that seem to operate in a non-Newtonian way? Is that possible, or do we now know everything that can be known? I'm sorry to tell you that even *suggesting* there might be other field systems as yet unknown is absolutely repugnant to many dogmatic scientists. They literally call it heresy.

It's a sad irony that *heresy* is a word and concept devised by orthodox religion and one that seems perfectly at odds with the open spirit of scientific inquiry. Perhaps Max Planck, who some call the Father of Quantum Physics, said it best, "Science advances one funeral at a time."

Biologist Rupert Sheldrake, perhaps my favorite heretic, has done more than anyone to bring the concept of morphic fields into both public awareness and the realm of scientific inquiry. This has made him extremely unpopular amongst Materialists, but when it comes to hacking reality, unseen forces of the non-supernatural type are worth exploring.

The Shape of Things to Come

According to Sheldrake, morphic fields are the memory banks of nature, providing the shape, structure and even behaviors for everything in our world.

Remember, there really is no physical matter as such. Atoms are *not* the smallest building blocks of matter. They may *act* like little billiard balls knocking into each other, but we know they aren't actually solid. To put it simply, atoms are made of energy, manifesting out of space.

And yet we experience the world, and our own bodies, as real, solid, physical objects consistent over time. Where do all these objects come from? How do the sub-atomic particles that make the atoms that make up the molecules that make up the objects know how to show up as a rock, or a typewriter, or a cactus or your pancreas?

Every object must have a sort of blueprint that holds its pattern – one that tells all of that energy how to coalesce into a particular shape. Those blueprints are held in the Field. Each blueprint is a subsidiary field within the master Field.

The overall morphic field for your body includes subsidiary fields for every part of your body. Your blood, your muscles, your bones. Every organ in your body has its own field that provides information not only for its structure but also its function. Not just the anatomy but also the physiology.

There's a blueprint for the individual cells of your liver, for example. But there's also a blueprint for the liver as an organ. Consider that the cells in your liver must all act simultaneously, in concert, to produce various enzymes. The field for your liver provides an epigenetic control system above and beyond the much slower intercellular communication.

Don't Fall In

About the time I was first learning about fields, I took my daughters to the San Francisco Aquarium. They were off looking at pretty jellyfish, so I was alone when I came upon a fairly large tank labeled Piranha and stopped to look. I'd never actually seen piranha before, and they really are rather frightening – big oversized mouths with scary-looking teeth.

As a kid, I'd seen movies where some hapless character fell in the river, and the piranha *got* him. The water would boil and churn, and within minutes they'd have him stripped down to bare bones. Piranhas were right up there with tornados, quicksand and black widow spiders, embodying the dangerous cruelty of Nature.

It occurred to me, watching about 20 of these scary looking fish swimming about randomly in their tank, that I really had no idea how accurate those Hollywood scenes might actually be. Certainly, the perils of quicksand had been overrated. Were these fish even dangerous at all?

Just as I was entertaining that thought, in that very moment, all 20 piranhas turned to face me. All of them. All together. Acting as one. It was sudden, and it was *terrifying*!

I'm sure a Materialist would have a ready explanation for their behavior – first one fish noticed me, and then a few other fish noticed that first fish was looking my way and then all the other fish began looking to see what those other fish were looking at and this just happened very quickly.

Rubbish. I'd been watching those fish intently, and they all turned together as *one*. I probably can't convey how scary that was. I literally jumped back – like about three feet back. Those piranhas were of one mind, and that Mind was clearly regarding me as food.

Have you ever seen a murmuration? Hundreds of thousands or even *millions* of starlings gather at dusk in great flowing, intricately coordinated patterns through the sky. A true aerial ballet. They move together so quickly and fluidly that it's easy to see that each bird is a participant in a greater field. The flock becomes a kind of temporary organism with a consciousness greater than the sum of its parts. A much gentler consciousness than the piranha!

Evidence of Morphic Fields

If morphic fields are the memory banks of nature, species make both withdrawals and deposits. We not only draw from them by downloading form and function but also upload new behaviors through repetition. This seems to parallel natural selection as a way of adapting to changing environments.

There are two well-documented examples of this I'd like to share with you here.

The Blue Tit

In Great Britain, the antics of a naughty little bird called the Blue Tit became widely known. Sometime in the 1920s, back in the days when the milkman would come around every morning to leave bottles of fresh milk on the doorstep, some cheeky little blue tit made an amazing discovery.

By pecking through the foil lids on the milk bottles, it could score some delicious cream. This began in Swaythling, a little suburb of Southampton. Other blue tits caught on and soon it was a problem around the town.

Strangely though, blue tits began doing this same trick in villages over a hundred miles away. This was perplexing since these birds rarely fly more than 15 miles from home. Thanks to newspaper accounts, and the British passion for bird-watching, the inexplicable spread of this cream-stealing behavior was carefully documented.

By 1927 the blue tit thievery had spread all across Britain, which was remarkable enough. Even more astonishing, the foil pecking behavior somehow jumped the English Channel over to Holland, Denmark and up into Sweden. Given their limited range, it was beyond belief that flocks of blue tits made that crossing. Even if one or two had been blown across in a gale, how did they instruct *all* of the continental blue tits *all at once*?

Then World War II broke out. In Holland, the German occupation shut down milk deliveries for eight long years. Blue tits only live for about 3 years. Can you guess what happened when the milk deliveries started back up after the war? Within a few months, all across Holland the blue tits were at it again. These were the grandchildren or great-grandchildren of the original tits.

Standard Materialist explanations simply can't account for this. So how *did* it happen? Initially, of course, the cream stealing behavior did spread through observation and imitation, however once enough blue tits were stealing cream, the repetition created enough 'resonance' to upload that behavior to the blue tit field. At that point, it became accessible to all blue tits everywhere.

This phenomenon is sometimes called the "hundredth monkey effect" after a 1982 book by Ken Keyes Jr. which referenced research by Japanese scientists in the 1950s studying macaque monkeys on the island of Koshima. Instead of stealing cream, the monkeys learned to wash their sweet potatoes. Once a critical mass of individuals, *the hundredth monkey*, caught on to this accidental discovery, immediately the learned behavior spread across the water to monkeys on other islands. Or so the story goes.

McDougal's Rats

An experiment in the 1920s by Harvard psychologist William McDougal inadvertently demonstrated this same effect. Generations of rats were taught to solve a water maze, and then carefully bred. The study was an attempt to determine whether learned behavior could be inherited genetically, even when the observation wasn't a factor.

The study did find that successive generations of rats could solve the maze with fewer and fewer mistakes on their first attempt. This remarkable discovery might have supported the theory of learned inheritance – except for one thing. Rats in the *control group*, whose parents had never learned the maze, saw the exact same improvements when they were run through the maze.

More surprising still, when the experiment was replicated in Australia, many of the rats knew how to swim the maze from the get-go, without any trial and error learning. They were genetically unrelated to the American rats from the McDougal study but somehow born knowing how to run the maze.

Without an understanding of morphic fields, there was really no way to explain what was happening. In both cases, the experiments were canceled, unpublished and all but forgotten! Sheldrake suggests that the rats that were forced to run McDougal's maze, again and again, uploaded the design of the maze to the morphic field for rats, where it became accessible to all rats.

I should mention that this was no ordinary maze. I'm sorry to report that it was extremely cruel and stressful. The rats had to swim or drown and had to learn to go against their nature, choosing a dark ramp over a lighted one at the end. The lighted ramp produced a painful electric shock.

It took some rats as many as 330 trials to solve the maze. And this was inflicted upon *32 generations of rats* over a 15-year period! I can't help but imagine the awful intensity of the experience, repeated over and over and over. The 'upload' came from both repetition and life or death urgency.

We've been taught to think of evolution as a strictly genetic process that happens through natural selection and thus takes a very long time. Of course, there's absolutely no doubt that natural selection happens. But the sharp dividing line between innate and learned behavior has become more an issue of doctrine than evidence.

Relatively fast changes in both behavior and form are likely driven by learned behaviors uploaded to the morphic field through repetition. This may account for at least some of the miracles of evolution, making a species *way* more adaptable to sudden changes in their environment.

In the next chapter, we'll take a look at human interactions with morphic fields – how they can keep us stuck and how to break free to live an intentional life.

CHAPTER 11

The Fields That Make You, You

When I was a teenager back in the '70s, there was a really cool looking sports car called the Bradley GT. It was actually made from a fiberglass shell that bolted onto a Volkswagen Beetle chassis. Seeing one on the road would bring a feeling of excitement, *"Wow! Look at that car!"* followed by total disappointment upon hearing the unmistakable and underwhelming sound of the VW engine.

Maybe this is a stretch, but you could almost say that humans are bolted onto a mammalian chassis. Whatever else we are, we're definitely animals, and lots of people go to some trouble to disguise that fact, shaving their faces, legs, and other areas, using deodorant or scents to hide any telltale animal smells. Certain religions even warn us of the perils of our 'primal instincts'.

Like it or not, we've got these animal bodies, and for the most part, they're great! Our basic biological fields for blood, bones, organs, skin, hair and such are pretty awesome. Aside from a few glitches with fight/flight/freeze, most of our mammalian physiology serves us really well. But we're not *just* mammals. It's our human *behavioral* fields where things get really interesting.

Humans are individuals. Some more than others, it's true. And some cultures are more collective than others. Compared with most animals though, we at least have the option to be individuals. That means each of us has our own individual morphic field that helps define our identity.

In much the same way that our body has nested fields for cells, organs and the overall organism, the field for our identity may include personal, familial, cultural, national, and possibly ethnic and religious fields that we're pretty much born into. We also have the more intentional fields we join. Professional fields, for example, such as medicine, law or plumbing. Or recreational fields, like being a 49ers fan, a stamp collector, or a deadhead.

If you're a heart surgeon, for example, you'll be plugged into the field for that profession, which is nested within the field of surgery, nested within the medical field. You might be Greek, or Korean, and attend church every Sunday, but spend Saturday nights as an avid swing dancer.

It's repetition that creates 'morphic resonance', so any highly developed, organized endeavor will likely have its own field. Religious rituals, in particular, can create extraordinarily strong morphic fields with the same gestures, words and songs repeated over and over for hundreds of years.

The Family Field

Of all the groups that influence our identity and beliefs, our own family is typically the strongest. Of course, many families are deeply tied into national, regional, cultural, professional and/or religious fields.

For better or for worse our family field provides the comprehensive context for our lives. Our mammalian heritage plays a role here – we're biologically programmed to find our place in the pack. We have an innate urge to belong. To fit in. The healthier our family, the more fluid our role can be, changing and adapting as the family changes. Roles can be shared or traded over time.

The more dysfunctional our family, the more rigid our role and the more we're just stuck with it.

The field of a family has a kind of life of its own. In my work with clients, I sometimes see that a grandparent's or even great grandparent's unresolved trauma is wreaking havoc on younger generations. It's as though the family field itself wants resolution and somehow drafts descendants to reenact events, even if they're unaware of the original trauma.

Patterns of abuse or neglect definitely get reenacted through the generations. Dad was molested and ended up molesting his own child – my client. She finds herself unlucky with partners – somehow attracting and choosing a boyfriend who ends up molesting her children.

Knowing that this sort of pattern can have its roots in the family field system, we're empowered to go looking for it there. There are ways of finding the originating events and ways of resolving them, often very quickly.

What is the Field?

There are all kinds of fields in physics, but as far as hacking reality goes, we're really interested in *the* Field, capital F. This is the great ocean where every morphic field is a wave, or drop of water.

Another name for it is 'the Matrix' or the Tao or the Mind of God. There's nothing that stands outside of The Field. You can't actually be apart from it, to observe it from the outside – although our human lives on Earth may be an attempt to approximate that experience.

Everything is connected within The Field, in the sense of quantum entanglement. From the time of the Big Bang, every subatomic particle is entangled as One. The Field seems to contain not only everything that is but everything that can be, which is the basis for quantum superposition.

Physicists often refer to '*a* quantum field' meaning the forces holding together those most minute nanoscopic vortices that seem to comprise all of what we know as matter. In that sense, a quantum field is just one indescribably tiny bit of the Universe, but The Field includes *all* levels of reality, on up to the ultimate macroscopic Universal level and perhaps multiple Universes at that.

Okay, but what does any of that have to do with you?

I think if you ask most people where memories are stored, they'll likely point to their head and say, "Memories are stored in the brain. Duh. Everyone knows that." Okay, they might not say "Duh," but they'd probably think it. Because yes, everyone *does* know that. And of course, everyone is wrong.

Quantum Mechanics has shown us that every event, every moment of our life is stored in The Field. Our memories are our own personal connection to those events – our access to them. Our brains *are* involved, but as receivers, not hard drives. They receive the broadcast that is us.

With near universal wifi and cloud storage, I think it's getting easier to understand this. I rarely dust off my old DVD collection – it's so much easier to just stream Netflix. And I used to have our photos printed at the drug store and then mail copies to my folks. Now I simply upload them to Facebook or Instagram, where all my friends and family can see them.

A few years ago a client told me a story that blew my mind and fundamentally changed my understanding of how all this stuff works. In the introduction, I mentioned Matrix Reimprinting, where I have my client imagine stepping into a memory and tapping on her younger self there. You may recall that we also change what happens and reimprint the new picture to replace or overwrite the original.

Jill and I had worked on a terrible memory that involved her two older brothers. Something bad happened to the three of them. I won't go into the details, but they were between 10 and 14 years old at the time. The new 'happy ending' picture we reimprinted was quite different than the original – a major upgrade.

Well, a few weeks later Jill called me up in a state of astonishment. She'd just returned from a family reunion where she'd seen her brothers, now in their late 50s. Quite spontaneously her brothers began talking about that troubling incident that she and I had worked on. She hadn't mentioned our session, or even that she was working with me.

To her utter amazement, her brothers began describing the new, positive, beautiful picture she and I had created! Their own memories of the event had completely changed. Somehow they were both remembering *our* new and very different picture.

Now how is that possible?

What Jill and I had done in her session was to access the actual traumatic *event* as it was stored in the Field and make changes to it. In computer terms, we'd hacked into cloud storage, opened up the original trauma file, *edited* the content and hit Save. Now anyone accessing that file will see our new and improved version. Which is what happened for her brothers.

The implications here are staggering. We can go far beyond simply accepting and adapting to what's happened to us, and through retrocausation, actually change them. Not only for ourselves but for others as well. In a sense, we're leveraging the quantum reality of superposition to open up a new timeline for our younger self in that memory, which tends to impact our current reality in wonderful ways.

And every moment of our lives is stored in The Field and potentially accessible, even back into the womb. The ones that hold the most promise for changing our lives are, of course, the really bad ones. Luckily for us, these are the easiest to access. We'll get into that more when we explore the Freeze Response. But next up, let's look at how fields interact with our genetic expression and the relatively new field of Epigenetics.

CHAPTER 12

Epigenetics: Hacking Your Genes

Have you ever noticed how many gene-related scientific breakthroughs cross your newsfeed each week? Just today I saw: "Schizophrenia breakthrough as genetic study reveals a link to brain changes."

You'd think by now we'd all be incredibly healthy, living for 150+ years, with zero depression, anxiety or any sort of mental illness whatsoever. There should be a pill to keep us effortlessly slim and fit and—on a personal note—I should definitely have a full head of hair. What's the holdup?

Tabloids and their sensationalist headlines aside, I've become very skeptical about bio-medical research focused on genes as the causal factor. I'm glad so many brilliant minds are working diligently to find a cure for mankind's urgent problems. I just think they're barking up the wrong tree.

It's a tree called Genetic Determinism. This is the theory that our genes control pretty much everything about us – physically, emotionally and behaviorally. Pick a problem, any problem – it's caused by bad genes. I'm pretty sure some version of Genetic Determinism is still being taught to school children, despite the fact that the theory met a sudden and unexpected death in the year 2000.

Bill Clinton was president then, and I still remember his big press conference announcing that the Human Genome Project had finally completed its groundbreaking work. After many years (and a *whole* lot of taxpayer funding) they'd successfully mapped the entire human genome for the first time. An exciting new frontier of scientific breakthroughs was opening up with the tantalizing promise of new cures for the incurable.

But there was a problem. A really big problem. Researchers had expected to find at least 100,000 genes, but probably closer to 140,000. This was considered the bare minimum to explain the enormous complexity of the human body.

Instead, they found around 30,000. That's about the same number of genes as a fruit fly.

Oops. Quite unintentionally, the Human Genome Project drove a great big holly stake right through the beating heart of Genetic Determinism. You don't have to be a professional biologist to realize the human body is fantastically more complex than a fruit fly's. If genes were actually running the show, they came up at least 100,000 short.

But it gets even worse. In the last 18 years since the big announcement, the number of human genes has been quietly revised down to less than 20,000!

How is this even possible?

Express Yourself!

It turns out that each gene can actually express itself in a number of different ways. If each gene could express in 10 different ways (and I'm totally making *that* number up), this would account for 200,000 variations. Diversity explained!

But what tells each gene how to express?

That's where this gets really interesting. It turns out that genes respond to signals from their environment, some of which are coming from outside of the cell the genes are part of. They'll express in different ways depending on the message they're receiving. This new idea is called *Epigenetics*, "Epi" in this case meaning "above." So rather than genes controlling everything, they themselves are controlled by external inputs.

Bruce Lipton pioneered this field, starting way back in 1967 with experiments demonstrating that genetically identical stem cells could become muscle, bone or fat cells depending on the environment in their respective Petri dishes. His book *The Biology of Belief* is highly recommended reading.

In those initial experiments, it was a chemical signal that determined how the stem cells would express, and we obviously have chemically based inter-cellular communication going on all the time in our bodies. But cells also receive and respond to energetic signals. Cells actually have antennas in their membranes to receive these signals. This is how they're able to act in concert, simultaneously, so that the various organs can do their jobs.

These energetic signals are absolutely influenced by our thoughts and beliefs. There's solid scientific proof of this – it's called the Placebo Effect. Our belief that a pill will cure us is often enough to do the job, even if the pill is just sugar or chalk.

Worry, anger, and heartbreak really *can* make us sick. Laughter and joy really *can* help us heal. Most of us probably have some personal experience of this. Or we've witnessed it in others. So, this should be obvious to all of us, right?

Unfortunately, most of us have been conditioned to disregard our own observations in favor of whatever we're being told by the experts. Genetic Determinism is an outgrowth of 19th-century Materialism which, as we've seen, holds that only matter is real and that consciousness is an inconsequential 'epiphenomenon' of brain chemistry and of no importance whatsoever to the functioning of the body.

From this point of view, thoughts and beliefs can't possibly matter. Your body is a machine. Sometimes it doesn't work correctly, and that's because of bad genes, injuries, or intrusions from dangerous pathogens. And these can only be addressed with corrective chemical or surgical interventions. End of story. If your dishwasher or DVD player is on the fritz, singing a happy song to it isn't going to fix it, right?

Your body is not a machine. Your body is a living organism. But Francis Crick, discoverer of the DNA helix, dubbed Genetic Determinism *"the central dogma"* back in 1958! It's the crown jewel of Materialism.

Organized Crime

Not to be *too* cynical, but there's another big reason why Genetic Determinism is still held up as valid science – corporate profits. Remember Bill Clinton's big press conference? Many of the honored guests there were heads of newly formed biotech companies who expected to capitalize on the publicly funded research.

Ever since then, the multi-national, multi-billion-dollar pharmaceutical industry has spent enormous sums keeping Genetic Determinism front and center in the media and in schools – most especially *medical* schools. The narrative that we're helpless victims of our bad genes has enabled them to sell us trillions of dollars of prescription drugs.

In the United States, we have a long history of suppression and persecution of non-pharmaceutical medicine, going back over 100 years. There is such endemic political corruption today that Danish researcher Peter Gøtzsche recently denounced Big Pharma as being organized crime. He meant that literally.

That might seem like an extreme statement, but did you know that pharmaceutical drugs are a leading cause of death in the developed world? They're tied with stroke for the #3 spot, right behind heart disease and cancer. A 2014 article from Harvard University ethics researcher Donald Light notes:

> *Few know that systematic reviews of hospital charts found that even properly prescribed drugs (aside from mis-prescribing, overdosing, or self-prescribing) cause about 1.9 million hospitalizations a year. Another 840,000 hospitalized patients are given drugs that cause serious adverse reactions for a total of 2.74 million serious adverse drug reactions. About 128,000 people die from drugs prescribed to them. This makes prescription drugs a major health risk, ranking 4th with stroke as a leading cause of death. The European Commission estimates that adverse reactions from prescription drugs cause*

200,000 deaths; so together, about 328,000 patients in the U.S. and Europe die from prescription drugs each year. The FDA does not acknowledge these facts and instead gathers a small fraction of the cases.

In researching this matter, I discovered there's actually serious debate on whether prescription drugs are the leading cause of death, or only third or fourth. This strikes me as a very strange debate to be having. Why are they on such a list at all?

I'm not trying to say that prescription drugs are bad. Antibiotics almost certainly saved my life a few years ago. And I'm not above taking ibuprofen if I have a terrible headache. But at the time of this writing, nearly 70 percent of Americans are on at least one prescription drug – and 50 percent are on two or more. One in six are on *psychiatric* drugs. Things are clearly out of balance.

Apart from that *whole leading cause of death* thing, there's another huge problem here – most drugs only treat or manage symptoms. Except for antibiotics, they don't actually *cure* anything. They don't fix the bad genes that are supposed to be causing the problems.

Bruce Lipton tells us that very few physical maladies are inherited genetically – less than 2 percent. The rest are likely caused by epigenetic signals resulting from unresolved traumas. If we're going to hack into the reality of illness, resolving those traumas is where the action really is. That means it's time to go exploring the deep, dark place where your traumas hang out - your subconscious mind.

CHAPTER 13

The Subconscious Mind

Imagine living in the same house your whole life. You know every square inch of it, but then one day there's a door you've never seen before, right in the corner of the living room. It looks like it's been there forever, but you'd swear it just suddenly materialized.

Opening the door, you see stairs leading down to a vast, dimly lit basement lined with countless shelves. And all of those shelves are crammed with old fashioned reel to reel tape decks. Thousands of them. The shelves stretch off into the dark unseen distance.

So you're just standing there looking at them, wondering what the hell this is all about when your phone starts ringing upstairs in the living room. And suddenly about six of the tape decks switch on, each one playing a different message over and over:

Hurry up and get the phone! It's rude to keep someone waiting
We're not expecting a call, are we? This must be bad news
Get it before the 5th ring!
Ugh. It's probably a salesman – don't pick it up!
You should really be calling mother more often, you know she's lonely
Don't pick up the phone, let a grown-up do that!

Welcome to your subconscious mind.

The subconscious has an important job. It's there to keep you safe. It does this by remembering and replaying – important messages are duly recorded and then switched on by current triggers. And this is totally automatic. There's no reference librarian down there to help prioritize the often conflicting messages.

The volume of the playback depends on the emotional intensity when the message got recorded. Even if that message is no longer relevant. Consider the *"Don't pick up the phone, let a grown-up do that"* recording. That's mom's voice when you were 3 or 4 years old. Why the hell is *that* still playing?

If mom was just playfully admonishing your 3-year old self, the recording is going to play a lot quieter than if she was yelling and followed it up with a slap. You may be 63 now, but when the phone rings and that tape starts playing, you might have some resistance to picking up the phone. Ringing phones may trigger unexplained anxiety.

Especially when another tape deck starts blaring, *"Hurry up and get the phone! It's rude to keep someone waiting."* Same yelling mom, but this one's from age 10. Now you've got two urgent tapes playing totally conflicting messages. Which one is louder?

When our tapes start playing, we tend to react emotionally. In fact, we begin feeling the emotions of the younger self from when they got recorded. Logically you know that it's safe to answer the phone. You may even know who is calling. Which makes the spike in anxiety quite perplexing, even alarming.

Running the Show

Many people have no idea they even have a subconscious mind. We're taught to believe that our conscious mind is all there is. In fact, many people believe they *are* their conscious mind. *I'm* the captain of my own ship. *I* make the decisions. *I'm* in charge.

Which is why procrastination and self-sabotage are so perplexing. I decided to lose weight, but somehow my hand is stuffing chocolate cake into my mouth! Who the hell is operating my hand? It's a little unsettling to realize we're actually on autopilot 98% of the time.

We know the subconscious is running our physical body. And more power to it! I *really* don't want to be running my digestive system, or regulating my blood pressure, secreting enzymes, repairing and replacing trillions of cells. I don't want to be involved with growing my eyebrows. I don't even monitor my breathing most of the time. It would be impossibly overwhelming.

The simple act of reaching for a glass of water involves a staggering number of coordinated movements by so many muscles and muscle groups. Input from both eyes has to be processed to create depth perception. The weight of the glass has to be estimated. Blood flow and nerve impulses have to be allocated.

When I choose to reach out for the glass of water that's a conscious decision, but really it's my subconscious mind that makes it happen with countless smaller decisions and actions below the level of my awareness. All of that stuff is subconscious, running on autopilot. A vast number of tape decks are dedicated to getting that glass of water to my lips.

So, the subconscious is running our incredibly complex physiology, fair enough. But what about our social interactions?

Social Programming

If you think about it, social rules are very complicated. It's easy to forget how crucial it was to get that stuff right, almost from birth. We're not born knowing *any* of this information instinctually. We have to learn what works with Mom and Dad through trial and error.

As infants, we're terribly helpless and dependent. Behaviors that seem to elicit the love and care we need are carefully recorded. And so are the actions that seem to provoke anger or neglect. Even in the womb, we may start developing beliefs about who we are and how we fit in.

And it's complicated! Behaviors that work with Mom may not go over well with Dad. Or something that works okay in the morning doesn't work at all late at night. Or two days later. The program needs constant revisions. Even in the best of circumstances with a warm, loving and consistent family, can you imagine the amount of processing required just in the first six months of life? It's *all* handled by the subconscious mind.

As you're reading or hearing these words, your brain is functioning in the Beta brain wave state, a 13-30 Hz frequency in which you're awake, focused, alert and capable of logical thinking. You're comparing what I've written with what you already know and believe in a rational process. Any assertions I make get vetted, in other words, and either accepted or rejected.

And young children can't do that! We don't have access to the Beta frequency for the first 6 or 7 years of life. Until then we're mostly in Theta and Alpha states, very connected to our inner world of imagination and daydreaming, but unable to think in a critical, rational way. We live in what's called a *hypnogogic state*, which means we're hyper-suggestible.

Picture a stage magician hypnotizing some hapless audience member into thinking he's a chicken. The poor fellow gets called up on stage, put into an Alpha brainwave state and is given a 'suggestion.' Now he's clucking about and flapping his elbows as if they are wings. Very amusing for everyone watching, but imagine being in that state for your first seven years!

Okay, say I'm 4 years old, and dad comes home after a really tough day. He's sitting at the dining room table bitterly complaining about how "an honest man can't get a break in this world, everyone's out to cheat you!" He punctuates this last statement by slapping the table in anger. Dad's usually pretty mellow, so this is clearly a big deal and very alarming.

As a four year old I'm not able to question what my dad is saying. I'm not thinking to myself, "Gosh, is that really true? *Everyone* is out to cheat you? Or is dad just having a really bad day for some reason?" I'm not thinking that because I can't. No Beta mind yet. I'm like a sponge soaking it all up. And anything with such a big emotional charge gets special attention.

Dad's message becomes one of the tape decks down in my basement and gets clicked on whenever issues of success or honesty come up. By the time I'm 30 I *know* that everyone is out to cheat me. That belief has been reinforced many times through many misinterpreted and reenacted events.

So now, years later, I've got a problem: An honest man *can't* be successful in this world. If I want to be a good person, and if that's really important to me, I'll need to avoid success like the plague! Conversely, if success is crucial for me, I may end up cheating other people *even if I didn't need to* because that's just how you do it.

The Core Glitch

If my program for reaching out to get a glass of water is flawed, the spilled water will provide clear and immediate feedback. The program will automatically self-correct and upgrade itself. Glitches in our social programming are a different story. Feedback is available, but it's often misinterpreted based on fundamental mistakes in our perceived reality.

Most of us can get through social interactions without a lot of thought or attention to what we're doing. But if our family was funky, that means our programming (which got installed to cope with them) might not work so well with normal folks.

The real culprit here is some sort of 'core belief' about ourselves. Instead of self-correcting, negative social feedback tends to simply reinforce these beliefs, leading to extreme self-consciousness, massive anxiety and all sorts of social problems. Situations that others navigate effortlessly can seem fraught with danger when our tape decks are blaring out warnings or admonitions.

Again, this comes from trying to adapt to our family. Children seem totally hardwired to blame themselves for whatever bad thing is happening. In the worst families, the parents agree! So, it's really our relationship with our own self at the core of the problem.

Examples of negative core beliefs include:
I'm unlovable – there's something wrong with me.
I have to be perfect to be loved.
I will be abandoned.
It's dangerous to relax/have fun/open up to others.
People can't be trusted.
The world is a dangerous place.
It isn't safe to be angry/sad/happy.

And so on...

Do you see how beliefs like these will color *every* experience? The more we really believe they're true, the more beliefs like these ruin our life. For example, if I absolutely *know* that I'm unlovable, then the only way I can have a relationship is to hide my true self. Even if I succeed and trick someone into loving my false front, they're not really loving *me*. So, no matter what I'll end up feeling lonely and unloved.

If my subconscious is running "I'm unlovable," I'll almost certainly choose a partner to confirm and reinforce that belief. I'd actually feel uncomfortable if I got together with someone who adored me – I'd likely be deeply suspicious of them, or else terrified of the inevitable rejection once they encountered the real me. Even if I slip up and choose a really great partner, I'll likely slip into self-fulfilling prophecy mode, becoming increasingly off-putting until I finally drive them away.

Even if I'm *aware* of what I'm doing, chances are I won't be able to stop myself. The compulsive power of the subconscious can be truly frightening. We say things like, "I'm my own worst enemy" or "I just can't help myself." We call it 'self-sabotage' but what's really going on here?

Just One Job

The number one job of the subconscious is to keep us safe. It does that by keeping things stable, running along like always, staying on course. Since we've survived this long, whatever we're doing must be working, and we'd better just keep doing it. That's what all those recordings are for.

At the same time, the bad stuff we've gone through is automatically projected onto the future. If we've suffered many rejections, we just *know* that's going to happen with our new partner. Last business crashed? This new one is sure to fail! We're kept 'safe' by feeling doomed!

Remember, there's no creative intelligence in the subconscious whatsoever. It's a bunch of damned tape decks, and all it can do is replay, repeat and re-enact. It doesn't matter how miserable that might make us. And it doesn't matter if circumstances have changed. It doesn't even matter if the same old behavior is going to kill us.

I've worked with clients who were obese to the point they were facing severe health risks. And yet they couldn't stop bingeing on junk food. Their relationship with food and eating was so entirely compulsive they were literally eating themselves to death. It's terrifying to be so out of control! Their 'autopilot' was taking them right over a cliff.

Hacking Reality means turning *off* the autopilot whenever it's not serving us. Otherwise, any change we want to make in our life is up against the subconscious mind. And honestly, all of our good intentions and will power just don't stand a chance against that basement full of tape decks.

In fact, we can go a step further. Instead of just turning it off, we can actually *reprogram* our autopilot. Change the tapes. We can reset the thermostat, so to speak, for our weight, our finances, intimacy with our loved ones, physical health, creative self-expression. You name it.

Once we re-align our subconscious mind with our actual hopes, dreams, and desires, achieving our goals can be as easy as reaching out for a glass of water. In the meantime, though, you may be sporting a few too many triggers that can switch those old tape decks on. In the next chapter, we'll look at what happens when the trigger registers as a threat.

CHAPTER 14

Fight or Flight

Monday morning, October 9, 2017. I wake up to my daughter pounding on my bedroom door. It's 4:30 am. As I struggle awake, I hear sirens. Lots of sirens. I smell smoke! My daughter says, "Dad, there's a fire. People are evacuating. You'd better get up."

She takes me out in front of the house, into the street. Hours before dawn the northern sky is glowing orange. There's an impossibly huge fire up on the hills and not far away. We hear explosions in the distance – propane tanks blowing up. The Santa Rosa Firestorm was raging and would burn for days unchecked.

That night 42 people died, and thousands of homes and businesses burned to the ground, most of this happening about ten minutes from my house. And it just *kept* happening for days. Tens of thousands of our neighbors were evacuated, and the air was thick with toxic smoke. It wasn't safe to be outside.

Our 'go bags' were packed and ready by the door. Every time we thought it was over, a new big fire seemed to flare up. Thousands of firefighters, police from other cities and the National Guard descended on Santa Rosa to subdue the fires and protect us from looters. This went on for 10 days, until finally, blessedly, we had a long drenching rain. By the end, 4658 homes had burned to ashes just in Santa Rosa.

The Stress Response

Whenever we're faced with a serious threat, the animal part of us reacts quickly and automatically. Adrenalized blood is shunted to our arms and legs so that we might run away or do battle. I could feel the tingle of it in my armpits and fingers, standing in the dark watching the blaze. It's not a pleasant feeling!

All of that extra blood has to come from somewhere. It gets requisitioned away from all the non-essential systems we really don't need if, for example, we're being chased by a tiger. Digesting our food is not a priority when we're at risk of being eaten ourselves. Same with healing cuts, bruises, and infections if we're about to be torn to pieces. Reproductive system? Forget about it!

Our wonderful neocortex is another system that gets downgraded during fight or flight. As much as 80 percent of the blood may drain away, effectively dropping our IQ into the basement.

Seriously, who needs higher reasoning, planning, and abstract thought when the *only* plan is to run like hell or scamper up a tree? We heard stories of neighbors who had only minutes to escape the firestorm grabbing random objects – a kitchen spatula or half a bag of pretzels while leaving their wallet or prescription drugs to burn.

During those 10+ days of the fire, I found it nearly impossible to get anything done. I couldn't make decisions or plans. We were all living moment by moment, endlessly searching online for the latest updates, but essentially paralyzed. This has given me new empathy for homeless people, or anyone trapped in poverty or a cycle of abuse. They're trapped because that executive part of their brain has simply shut down.

Humans are special. It takes a genuine existential threat to snap other animals into fight or flight. Something really *is* out to get them. But we humans only have to imagine it. Our limbic brain can't seem to tell the difference and reacts just the same.

And for humans it doesn't even have to be physical peril – a threat to our identity can be enough. The 'happily married' wife discovers her husband is cheating on her. The ambitious salesman is expecting a promotion but gets handed a cardboard box and told to clear out. Hello fight or flight.

This is a really big problem for humans in this modern world. Fight or flight evolved to be a *short-term* survival mechanism. Assuming we do survive and get to safety, everything in the body returns to normal, and life is sweet again. But not if the perceived 'threat' is ongoing.

Adrenaline is a key ingredient in the rocket fuel that powers fight or flight. Oddly enough, our adrenal glands also make another crucial hormone, DHEA. This is the 'growth hormone' necessary for building new cells to replace the old, worn out ones. We're talking about *billions of cells* that need to be replaced daily.

Unfortunately, our adrenal glands can't make both hormones at the same time. Routine maintenance is an extremely low priority if you're running from that tiger. You need all the adrenaline you can get, so everything else has to wait. Bruce Lipton puts it this way – we're either in growth mode or survival mode. They're mutually exclusive.

This is why chronic stress of being stuck in fight or flight is such a killer. It really means *deferred maintenance*. In other words, our body can't repair itself fast enough. This sets the stage for illness and strongly contributes to the record levels of degenerative disease we see in modern times.

Lucky for us we have EFT.

Tapping Away Stress

EFT (Meridian Tapping), which I briefly discussed in the introduction, is a powerful modality for shutting off fight or flight, dramatically lowering stress levels and removing triggers that keep switching it back on. Later in the book, I'll present a crash-course in how to use this amazing tool, but for now, let's take a look at how it actually works in your body.

The amygdala is the part of your brain that handles stress and fight or flight. It monitors the steady stream of information coming in through your senses, comparing all the bits and pieces to a memory bank of all the bad things you've experienced or witnessed. Whenever there's a seeming match, the amygdala turns up the volume on your stress response or actually throws the switch to go into full-on fight or flight.

All of this happens in your limbic (mammalian) brain, which evolved millions of years before our wonderful human speech centers. This means the amygdala doesn't actually register spoken language.

Let me say that again: the part of our brain that controls stress and fight or flight is *non-verbal*. Words don't register. This is why traditional "talk therapy" is largely ineffective for so many issues, especially any kind of trauma.

Imagine telling a Vietnam vet with PTSD, "Hey man, chill out! The war's over. You're home now. You're totally safe, just relax." Would that be helpful? Of course not. The part of his brain that understands what you're saying is true *isn't in charge* of the stress. His amygdala calls the shots, and it can't understand or register the meaning of your words.

What it *does* register is tapping.

Tapping with our fingers on certain key acupuncture points tells the amygdala that whatever we're focusing on is no longer a threat. The stress response is rapidly dialed down and fight or flight is switched off. The stimulus is decoupled from the response – triggers disappear. Our system relaxes and begins to regulate again. And this can happen very quickly.

The limbic brain is the key player here. Talk therapy tries to reach it in a top-down way, through the cerebral cortex which is where our words live. EFT on the other hand, reaches up through the lower, reptilian brain which is all about touch and motion.

When we're rhythmically tapping on the body, this seems to provide a clear and immediate message to the reptilian brain that all is well. And this is communicated directly to the amygdala.

Ironically the words we use in EFT are mainly intended to elicit the distress – just the opposite of talk therapy. We name what's wrong as specifically as possible so that the tapping can de-couple what we're focusing on from the amygdala's memory bank of bad, scary things. It really works!

If you can't wait to try it out for yourself, go ahead and jump to my EFT Crash Course (Chapter 21). Otherwise, let's keep going! In the next few chapters, we'll explore just what happens when Fight or Flight fails, and the Freeze Response kicks in.

CHAPTER 15

The Freeze Response

I used to live in a funky little place out in the country with my wife and our two cats. One night we woke up to strange snuffling sounds in the living room. Flipping on the light, we saw a big old possum waddling across the floor, headed for the cat food. That was one fat possum, so I guess he'd been coming through the cat door and helping himself for some time.

This was 3 a.m. on a chilly September night and my first close encounter with a possum. They are truly strange creatures! Most people consider them very ugly, with their long rat tail, coarse, dirty looking hair and beady eyes. I certainly wasn't pleased to have this big ugly creature in my living room.

My impromptu strategy was to open the front door, grab a broom and try to shoo the thing out. The possum had other ideas. He tried to frighten me by showing his mouth full of pointy teeth – which worked pretty well! But when I persisted with the broom, he crawled under a table and flopped over on his side, like a dead thing.

I'd heard the term 'playing possum,' but I'd never actually seen it in real life. The damn thing just lay there, inert. Mindful of all those sharp looking teeth, I finally put on my thickest coat and a pair of work gloves and picked him up by the tail. I totally expected him to suddenly thrash around and try to bite me, but I needn't have worried. That possum was dead to the world.

Dangling the creepy old thing by his tail, I carried him outside and laid him down under some bushes. Despite the chill, I stayed out there for a few minutes, wondering if it would get up and waddle off.

Nope. I finally gave up and went back to bed, but he was gone in the morning.

You might wonder how 'playing possum' could be any kind of survival strategy. It turns out most predators are reluctant to eat dead animals they come across. Who knows how long that thing's been lying there? Old dead meat might be rotten and make them very sick, so they tend to just leave it alone.

I want to point out though; the possum isn't *deciding* to play dead. It's not choosing this response. 'Playing possum' is an entirely involuntary reaction that kicks in when there's no apparent way for Fight or Flight to work. Biologists call this the Freeze Response.

If you've ever seen a possum ambling along, you can guess they're not adept at flight. And except for me, those sharp teeth aren't really fooling anyone. Possums are pretty ugly, but they're the opposite of ferocious, and so they've become the poster child for The Freeze Response.

Built for Speed

Unlike the possum, impalas are very fast indeed. Living in great herds on the plains of Africa, they're adept at flight. That said, it's safe to say that no impala ever died of old age. Their herds are surrounded by lions, hyenas, and cheetahs, just waiting for a meal. A meal that's liable to happen whenever an impala starts to slow down even just a little.

So, impalas spend their entire lives under constant threat of being run down, torn apart and eaten. That sounds a bit stressful, doesn't it? Given that human beings are prone to any number of stress-related diseases, one might expect impala to be a rather sickly bunch. But of course, they're not.

Why not? Why don't wild animals get the same stress diseases we do? Our pets get them, and so do zoo animals. What's so healthy about living wild? That was a question posed by psychologist and body-mind pioneer Peter Levine. His 1997 book, *Waking the Tiger*, explores a possible answer.

Levine actually filmed impala with high-speed movie cameras and discovered something interesting – whenever the race was clearly lost, and the cheetah's claws were about to sink into her haunches, the impala would collapse. And this would happen *before* contact was made.

This is the Freeze Response, kicking in when flight had clearly failed. Levine observed that sometimes instead of eating it on the spot, the cheetah would instead drag the impala off to some bushes and then leave to go round up her cubs for dinner. Left alone long enough, the impala would suddenly jump up and hightail it back to the herd!

But just before it went back to munching grass, that impala would do one more thing. It would shake. It would shake and shake and shake. Levine came to realize that the shaking was basically running in place. It was releasing the massive amounts of Flight energy that had become trapped in the impala's muscles during the instant of Freeze.

Levine realized this Freeze Discharge was a necessary step for returning to normal, and that it would actually *increase* an animal's resiliency in the face of a new threat. It's Nietzsche's "that which does not kill us makes us stronger" principle. But *only* if we're able to shake it off.

The Drop of a Pin

We humans basically share the same limbic brain as possum and impala. We experience Fight or Flight in much the same way and lacking any great talent for fighting or fleeing, we're a bit more on the possum end of the spectrum and apt to go into the Freeze Response rather easily.

There are four main triggers for the Freeze Response:
1. A threat (real or perceived)
2. Perceived helplessness in the face of the threat
3. Surprise or shock, we didn't see it coming, it came out of the blue
4. A feeling of isolation – no one's there for us, no one has our back

Children and babies are especially prone to the Freeze Response. Not only are they genuinely helpless, but lacking experience of life they're easily surprised and scared. And when one of their caretakers is the source of the threat, the sense of isolation is powerful. They can go into Freeze at the drop of a pin.

I have a whole collection of photos showing terrified young children encountering the Easter Bunny or Santa Claus for the first time, desperately looking to their laughing parents for help. Complete and total Freeze Response.

Humans are special, of course. We don't need actual danger – a threat to our *identity* can do the trick. Being scolded by an angry parent who tells us we're a bad little boy or girl can absolutely trigger the Freeze Response, even when there's no spanking or physical harm. Even the sudden, unexpected withdrawal of attention from a normally loving parent can throw a child's sense of belonging into chaos, triggering the Freeze.

Unlike other animals then, our moments of Freeze rarely come from being chased by dangerous animals. Our Freeze Response is generally triggered by complex social situations – being yelled at by Mom or Dad, for example. Simply shaking the energy out of our muscles, impala style, doesn't seem to do the trick.

The biological imperative to 'shake it off' is still there, but since we can't reenact the motions of fight or flight, our subconscious sets up similar social situations for us, again and again. We find the same sort of bully keeps showing up. Or we keep getting into the same sort of dysfunctional relationships. We'll be looking at this in more depth in the chapter on reenactment.

First though, let's examine what actually happens in our brain whenever the Freeze Response is triggered.

CHAPTER 16

The Trauma Capsule

As far as your brain is concerned, going into the Freeze Response is a really big deal. Fight or Flight has failed, which suggests to our more primitive limbic brain that we're about to be killed! As discussed in the last chapter, this can happen even if it's just our identity that's threatened and we're not in any actual danger.

But your brain can't tell the difference, so anytime you go into Freeze the memory of the event is stored in a very special way. If you do survive, remembering every detail may help you avoid the danger in the future, or at least improve your reflexes if you do.

Fender Bender

Have you ever been in a fender bender? Sort of like bumper cars only much more expensive? Collisions like this don't usually mess us up too badly. You might get a little banged up, maybe a touch of whiplash, but after a few days or a week or two you'll be right as rain if you're lucky.

Turns out not everyone is so lucky. Dr. Robert Scaer is a neurophysician who ran a pain clinic in Boulder, Colorado. Over the years he'd see patients develop severe, debilitating symptoms from accidents that wouldn't really harm most people. The insurance companies would claim fraud, of course. These patients, with no real physical basis for their exaggerated injuries, were just faking it to get a big fat settlement.

They had a point. Medically, there shouldn't have been a real problem. But if a patient was faking, then once the settlement came through there should be a miraculous recovery, right? That's not what Dr. Scaer witnessed. His patients would more often keep getting worse and worse in a downward spiral of disability. It was a frustrating mystery.

No apparent physical cause meant no effective treatment. And this was not a rare occurrence. Or not rare enough.

Luckily for us, Dr. Scaer happened to come across Peter Levine's book *Waking the Tiger* and the concept of the Freeze Response. He began to investigate the early experiences of his mystery patients and discovered that *all* of them had experienced major childhood traumas. Being an experienced neurophysician, Dr. Scaer was able to understand the complex workings of the human brain at that critical moment when the Freeze Response is triggered.

He presented his findings, observations, and speculations in a series of books. The first two are frankly tough for laypeople to get through, but his third book *Eight Keys to Brain Body Balance* is an absolute treasure. It's genuinely readable and highly recommended. I'll try my best to summarize some of the main ideas here.

The Trauma Capsule

At the moment of Freeze, our brain takes a snapshot of both our internal and external environments and stores this information in a particular kind of memory bank.

The external snapshot contains all the information pouring in through your senses– sights, sounds, smells, the breeze on your skin, a taste in your mouth, temperature and humidity, the sensation of flying through space in a car crash. Normally our brain automatically filters out almost all of this stuff, since most of it is totally irrelevant to whatever we're focusing on. In Freeze though, it's all there.

Our internal snapshot records what we're feeling emotionally, which given the circumstances, is likely to be negative and overwhelming – fear, grief, anger or rage, despair. The brain also records whatever we're thinking to make sense of what's happening to us – more on this later.

Learning to Ride a Bike

When you were a kid, did you learn to ride a bike? If so, let me ask you a question. Say you hadn't ridden a bike for years and years do you think you'd be able to get back on a bike and ride it? I've asked a lot of people that question and all of them know they could. Even if it's been decades. Here's the thing: that's not because you'd remember how to ride a bike. It's because *you never forgot*. Do you see the difference?

The knowledge of how to ride a bike is stored in what's called *procedural memory*. It's kept current, for immediate access, much like RAM on your computer. Anything stored in procedural memory is always *on*. And our Freeze Response memories are stored in exactly the same way.

For us, they're just memories, but for our body and subconscious, they're current events. In other words, they *never stop happening*! Let that sink in.

The Capsule

Dr. Scaer coined the term 'Trauma Capsule' to include not only the contents (the internal/external snapshot) but also the container for the experience. If you picture an actual capsule, there's the shell and then what's inside. The shell of a trauma capsule is composed of dissociation.

By dissociation, I mean that we're protected from awareness of the contents of the capsule – especially from the raw emotional intensity of the experience. We literally 'dis-associate' from it. It's held somewhat apart from our conscious mind as a way of enabling us to just get on with our life. Otherwise, we might remain paralyzed or simply lie down on the ground and give up.

To the extent the capsule is working we may not remember the event at all. In other words, total amnesia. I've had clients with no childhood memories whatsoever before the age of 8 or even 12 years old. The memories are actually there, but they had so many trauma capsules; there was a wall of dissociation occluding them.

More commonly though, we *do* remember that something happened but it's a bit fuzzy, or the feelings are somewhat muted. A client will tell me: "I remember my grandfather molested me, but I don't have any feelings about it, so I guess it wasn't a big deal." Nope. It *was* a big deal, and the feelings are definitely there in full force–she's just being protected by the encapsulation of the experience.

So two things going on here with the trauma capsule – we're protected from awareness of the experience, but at the same time, it never stops happening. And that means it's never resolved, never healed. And sometimes the capsule leaks.

The Leaking Capsule

Have you ever met someone who just rubbed you the wrong way? Maybe it's their tone of voice or a certain facial expression. Or you might have no idea what it is, but somehow they just bug the hell out of you. We tend to assume there's something wrong with that person, and maybe there is. Perhaps our intuition is just warning us.

Then again, what if they just happen to have the same unusual facial expression as Mrs. Nasty, your third-grade teacher who always gave you such a hard time. So much so that you've got a few trauma capsules starring her as the perpetrator. And now some of those awful third grade feelings are leaking into you every time you encounter this new person (who might actually be very nice.).

There's a very good chance you won't connect the dots and remember Mrs. Nasty and third grade. We naturally assume the feelings we're experiencing are our feelings in the present, even when they're leaking into us from a younger self.

Perhaps the most extreme example of this is having a panic attack. Some sight, sound or smell from one's current environment happens to match the contents of an old trauma capsule. Instead of leaking though, the capsule totally ruptures, and feelings of terror come flooding in, usually for no apparent reason.

The lack of any clear or obvious threat only serves to amplify the panic – someone having a panic attack often thinks they're going crazy. And without any obvious cause, there's nothing external they can change to make it all better. They don't know how to avoid or prevent another bout, which leaves them feeling powerless and despairing. This experience is *so* horrible that fear and anxiety themselves become triggers, in the ultimate self-fulfilling prophecy.

In my work, the starting point in eliminating panic attacks is to firmly identify the source of the emotions. It's kind of a weird idea at first, but I have my clients tap on the statement:

Even though I have this terrible fear, these are not my feelings – they belong to a younger self. There's nothing happening right now to warrant these feelings at all. These feelings belong to a younger self. She's absolutely terrified, and her feelings are coming right into my body. But I know that she's going to make it, that she'll be okay, and that whatever is happening is not her fault. She's a great kid, and I'm going to help her. But I can't help her if I am her. I give myself permission to close down the open channel between us until I feel strong enough to really help her.

And it's not always a panic attack. This experience of being emotionally hijacked by a younger self happens to most of us fairly often. Anytime we're having disproportionate or inexplicable feelings this is almost certainly what's going on. A trauma capsule is leaking.

A Shock to Our System

Whenever we encounter a really stressful life experience, it takes energy to cope with it. Moving house, for example. Or the death of a loved one. Losing our job, or even getting a nice promotion. Getting married. Or divorced!

It also takes energy to keep those trauma capsules sealed up. And the more distressing the memory, the more energy that's likely required. So dealing with a really stressful situation can sometimes tax enough of our energy that some of the capsules breach.

For Dr. Scaer's patients, going through a fender bender was enough to breach one or more capsules. It's worth noting that the current stressor may be totally unrelated to the feelings being released. Automotive trauma isn't really a match for the childhood sexual abuse of Dr. Scaer's patients. The pain and hassle of the accident just took too much energy out of their system.

Our subconscious mind pretty much hates these trauma capsules. They're like ticking time bombs or dangerous cysts that need to be gotten rid of. In the next chapter on reenactment, we'll look at the amazing and disastrous strategy our subconscious uses to accomplish this.

CHAPTER 17

Reenactment

The subconscious mind is a one-trick pony. Really the *only* thing it can do is repetition. Remember, there's no creative mind there, just banks of tape recorders getting switched on by current events, but always playing the same old tape loops. That said, it's incredibly good with that one trick.

I'd like you to consider the possibility that just about any bad thing that happens to you in your adult life may be a reenactment of some childhood Freeze Response moment. If the bad thing keeps happening, again and again, it's *definitely* a reenactment.

In the last chapter, I mentioned how uncomfortable our psyche is with all those trauma capsules. It wants them gone. If you were an impala you could just shake your leg muscles and discharge all that energy. You'd be reenacting running away from the cheetah. That's the same biological imperative at work with us, only our Freeze Response more often comes from social situations than being chased by a predator.

Have you ever known someone who kept hooking up with the same sort of bad partner? Maybe they keep marrying someone who cheats on them, or turns out to be an alcoholic or needing to be rescued, or even abusive. Even when they're vetting the new potential partner so carefully, they get fooled again. It almost sounds like an urban legend, but it's shockingly common.

And it's not just choosing a partner. I've had clients who were rear-ended while at a stoplight five times in a few years. Or the same kind of bully keeps showing up. Or every investment they make is a disaster. The classic question in EFT is, "What does this remind you of?" and it almost always goes back to pre-7 years old.

These recurring events are the subconscious mind at work, doing its best to discharge that Freeze Response. Unfortunately, this never seems to work. The energies of Fight and Flight are not discharged. Instead, it just makes everything worse, by reinforcing our perceptual filters and building up an oppressive feeling of inevitability. The morphic field around the pattern is actually strengthened by repetition.

It's so frustrating being caught up in this sort of repeating pattern. I've noticed people can get really excited when I start talking about this stuff – "You mean you can make it *stop*?! Shut up and take my money!"

The good news is that understanding the Freeze Response and how our subconscious reenacts early childhood traumas can lead us to the source. The even better news is we now have ways of resolving those early traumas once and for all.

Wormholes

Imagine you're standing at one end of a long corridor, representing the timeline of your life. Looking down this corridor means looking into your own personal history. Way down at the furthest end there you are in the womb. In between though, the corridor is lined with countless framed photographs, each one a memory, depicting some event in your life.

Walking down that corridor, you'll notice some of the frames don't actually hold photographs. Instead, there's a kind of hole in the wall. Looking through one of these holes you see an actual event playing like a videotape loop over and over. Except it's a perfect life-size 3D holographic representation.

Each one of these holes in the wall opens onto a moment you went into Freeze. Here's your 8-year-old self, listening to Mom and Dad arguing and realizing they're getting a divorce. There's that time you failed the spelling test in 2nd grade, and the whole class laughed at you. These are your trauma capsules.

Peter Levine suggests the Freeze Response creates a wormhole through our normal space-time experience. That's what makes the hole – perhaps because of the way our brain stores the experience in procedural memory where it never stops happening.

Unlike the framed 2D photographs, you can actually step *through* one of these holes and totally be there, in that scene, either stepping into the body of your younger self and merging with them, or staying in your current adult consciousness so that now there are two of you there – you *and* your younger self. This latter approach is the basis for Matrix Reimprinting. As our adult self in the scene, we can actually communicate with and help our younger self.

Remember the Ghost of Christmas Past from the movie, *Scrooge*? He takes Ebenezer Scrooge back to certain key moments in his life where bad decisions took him down a dark path. Poor old Ebenezer only got to watch it all unfold. With Matrix we help our younger selves get out of Freeze and empower them, creating a positive new outcome. Essentially we create a new memory that overwrites the old one, reversing the negative beliefs we got stuck with.

Trauma capsules do give us one silver lining – thanks to the wormhole effect, it's incredibly easy to locate and step into these events. And thanks to EFT and Matrix Reimprinting, it's wonderfully easy to rewrite them. We do this not only to stop being hijacked (which in itself is wonderful) but also to change our programming, which can have even more profound ramifications.

What Did You Decide?

So far, we've looked at how our brain creates a 'snapshot' when the Freeze Response hits and how the intense emotions in the trauma capsule can leak out, effectively hijacking us. But there's another incredibly important part of that snapshot – the answer to the question our younger self was asking, "Why is this happening to me?"

Their answer to that question was really a decision, either about themselves or about how the world is. They might have decided *this is happening because I'm unlovable* or, *this is happening because the people you trust will always turn on you.* The younger we are at the time, the more illogical our decisions tend to be. Even the smartest little kid has very little experience to draw from.

On top of that, children are basically hardwired to make *everything* their fault. This is a way of trying to control unacceptable events at a time when we're relatively powerless.

This isn't just being egocentric. If the bad thing is happening because I'm a bad kid, then maybe there's some way *I* can change and make it all okay. Maybe I can somehow stop being bad, and then Mom and Dad will be happy and get along.

We also make decisions about the world – it's a dangerous place, men can't be trusted, marriage is hell, no one really loves anyone, something bad always happens, it's not safe to be happy, it's not safe to trust anyone. Can you imagine how debilitating beliefs like these must be?

Whatever we decide in the moment of Freeze becomes a belief that, from that moment on, serves as a kind of perceptual filter. This belief begins to change our expectations of how the world is and what we can expect out of life. And because we tend to see what we expect to see, we're prone to misinterpreting subsequent events in a way that reconfirms our beliefs. Believing is seeing.

At some point our behavior adapts to these negative expectations, setting the stage for self-fulfilling prophecies. Karl Dawson, the creator of Matrix Reimprinting, says, "We're always looking for evidence that what we believe is true." And sure enough, we find it.

This happens not only through misinterpreting events, but also thanks to the terrible subconscious strategy of reenactment. The negative, limiting beliefs we acquire through moments of Freeze become the bars of our self-made prisons. Hacking reality often comes down to swapping out those beliefs – it's our 'get out of jail free' card!

Let's look a little more deeply at the reality of our younger selves, trapped in their moments of Freeze and how we can help them.

CHAPTER 18

Your Younger Self is Real

Once upon a time a man sent his wife to me hoping I could fix her. She wanted to divorce him, so obviously she was crazy. He hoped I could help her chill out and stop being so ridiculous. Alas, the outcome wasn't quite what he'd hoped for.

The wife – I'll call her "Sarah" – had a somewhat different perspective on the situation: Her husband was a total jerk, and after ten years she was *done* with his controlling behavior and corrosive verbal abuse. Now in her early 60s, he was just the latest in a long line of awful husbands and terrible boyfriends.

Sarah wanted to know why all of her romantic relationships had been so consistently bad. And, was there any hope of ever having a good one, or was being alone the only solution.

Intelligent, educated, attractive and capable, and with a long successful career, why would Sarah have chosen these men who treated her so poorly? After one or two bad ones, why couldn't she spot them coming a mile away and pick someone nice?

To find the root of her relationship woes I had Sarah do what I like to call 'The Magic Trick.' I had her tap on her collarbone point (one of the EFT points we'll explore in Chapter 21) and ask this question: "Show me an image of my younger self where this pattern began for me." I let her know it didn't need to be a full-on memory, just a glimpse of her younger self. And it didn't need to make any sense – we need the rational mind to take a backseat here.

Sarah was surprised to see an image of herself as a toddler, around two years old, home alone with mom on a sunny afternoon. Mom was sitting on the couch, and the little girl climbed up to snuggle with her.

It always felt nice and reassuring and lovely, snuggling up to mom. But not this time. For some reason Mom turned away, giving the little girl the cold shoulder. Then Mom got up and walked out of the room

This image made no sense at all to Sarah. It wasn't something she'd ever remembered before. What did *this* have to do with anything? The little girl just sat there, and Mom left the room – big deal. Someone watching this might not have even noticed anything happened.

Over the years I've learned to trust The Magic Trick absolutely – *especially* when the image makes no sense. So, I had Sarah imagine stepping into that scene as her adult self and take the little 2-year-old's hand. The little girl was frozen in shock, but we were able to do EFT tapping on her.

I had Sarah ask the little girl what she'd decided about herself at that moment. Can you guess what the 2-year-old told us?

"I'm unlovable and will be rejected."

Though there were important events later in life, this was the actual genesis of Sarah's bad relationship pattern.

In Matrix Reimprinting we call Sarah's 2-year-old younger self an ECHO, which stands for Energetic Consciousness Hologram and is something like an 'inner child' only not necessarily a child and not exactly 'inner' as ECHOs exist in our energy fields more than our bodies.

Remember how the Freeze Response creates a trauma capsule? Well, that's where the ECHOs live, endlessly reliving the threat of whatever terrible experience triggered Fight or Flight, along with their feelings of helplessness, shock, and isolation which sent them into Freeze.

For Sarah's younger self it was a total surprise when Mom pulled away. That had never happened before, and she was suddenly alone. At the very least, this was a threat to her identity as the beloved little daughter. Being so young though, it may have seemed an existential threat – who will take care of me? Will I die now?

Also, Sarah's little 2 year old had no real resources to deal with the situation – she could barely put a sentence together. Then when mom walked out her sense of isolation was total, and she went right into Freeze.

Whenever the Freeze Response hits, a part of us splits off to contain the intensity of the experience. This part of us is the ECHO, a holographic chip off the old block, so to speak. It's actually an exact duplicate of our consciousness at that moment in time, made of energy and consciousness.

For us, the experience becomes a memory. For the ECHO it's a current event that never stops happening.

We go on to learn and grow and change with all of our subsequent experiences, but the ECHO never changes. The more time goes by for us, the more our consciousness will diverge from the ECHOs.

Another way to put this is that an ECHO has an *independent* consciousness from our adult self. We're not just imagining them or making them up – ECHOs are real.

ECHOs Are Real

I learned all this from Karl Dawson, but never really *got* it until I worked with a woman in the Midwest. She was in Michigan but had grown up in Russia. I remember she had a lovely accent. We were working on a memory where her younger self was about five years old.

I had my client step into the scene, take the little girl's hand and introduce herself. I was still pretty new to Matrix work so what happened next was a total surprise. My client said,

"She isn't answering me. She's just standing there."

So I asked, "Is she aware of you?"

"Oh yes, she's looking right at me! She looks confused."

This had never happened before, and at first, I had no idea what to do (I may have been panicking a bit). Then it hit me.

"Are you speaking to the little girl in English?"

"Yes"

"Can you speak to her in Russian?"

"Sure"

And then we were off and running. My client's younger self didn't understand English! She wouldn't learn it for at least five more years.

I knew my client didn't make this up. She was at least as surprised as I was, and also, she was paying me! She wouldn't waste valuable session time fooling around. This taught me that ECHOs *are* actually real, at least in the sense of having an independent consciousness.

I had this happen a few more times – with Norwegian, German and Chinese clients. Now, of course, I just have my client speak to their younger self in their native tongue.

Captain Kangaroo?

Sometimes clients worry that they're making the whole encounter up in their heads, that it's just a fantasy in their imagination. Which might still be therapeutic, but then their younger self will say or do something totally surprising!

For example, my client *knows* her ECHO is terribly sad, she's always known that. But when asked, her younger self says she's actually pissed off. One of those "Wait, what!?" moments.

I remember having a client ask her ECHO how she'd like the situation she was in to change – her eyes flew open in astonishment. My client literally said

"What the f***? She says she wants Captain Kangaroo to read her a bedtime story while she falls asleep! *Captain Kangaroo*?! I haven't thought of him since I was 5 years old!"

"And how old is your younger self?"

"Oh... Right... She's 5 years old!"

I never get tired of witnessing these exchanges, because there's something so cool in realizing these ECHOs are real. Cool because we can actually help them, tap away their distress and get them into a happier picture.

The downside is, without our help, they never seem to heal and never go away. We may forget the memories they inhabit – but our

ECHOs are always right there under the surface of awareness, waiting to be triggered.

The Open Channel

Whenever we're experiencing intense negative emotions that are disproportionate to our actual circumstances, it's a safe bet that those feelings are really coming into us from a younger self, trapped endlessly reliving some awful experience. Some trigger has caused a breach in the dissociation of the trauma capsule, and suddenly we're feeling feelings that aren't really ours.

Which is a weird thought, isn't it? I might be feeling the feelings of my 3-year-old younger self, who just got knocked down by a wave at the beach, or is watching his sister get spanked. Those feelings might be really intense, but they're not *my* feelings. They're his.

That 3-year-old is definitely a part of me, but 56 years later I've had a few experiences, learned a thing or two. I'm actually in a pretty strong position now to help my younger self. For example, I know that however bad things are for him, he's going to survive – I'm living proof of that! I also know that whatever is happening isn't his fault.

Sometimes a channel opens up between you and a younger self. Her feelings can leak into you, or come flooding in. But that channel runs both directions, and it's totally possible to send love, compassion, and encouragement back down the channel to her.

The feelings that come flooding into us from our ECHOs can be extremely unpleasant, especially when we don't understand what's happening. It's understandable that people may try really hard to shut down these open channels. Sugar, alcohol, pot, narcotics, antidepressants, sex, gambling, shopping and all sorts of other compulsive behaviors can do the job, temporarily. And of course, those behaviors can cause all sorts of problems in our lives.

We now have ways of actually *helping* our younger selves, thanks to Matrix Reimprinting. We can liberate them from the endless loop of the trauma capsule they inhabit. Their old feelings of fear, rage, shame, and sorrow are gone, so they can't hijack us anymore. Instead, they can become a source of joy and empowerment.

Full Circle

Remember Sarah's 2-year-old, alone back on the couch? Once we'd done some tapping to get her out of shock, we set about changing the picture. We asked Mom why she was so cold to her little daughter, and why she walked away. She told us she'd just gotten off the phone after getting some really bad news from her sister.

Mom was really surprised her little daughter was upset! She let her know it wasn't her fault at all and she was so sorry to have freaked her out! They ended up snuggling on the couch after all and the little girl's belief that she was unlovable and would be rejected just melted away, replaced by a lovely sense of being valued and respected. That's the new picture we reimprinted.

Sarah went on to divorce her husband and felt *great* about it. Her relationship with herself had changed, and she decided to be single for a while, to get more and more comfortable with this new identity of being lovable before finding a new mate.

Put another way, helping Sarah's little 2-year old self get what she needed freed adult Sarah from subconscious reenactment, so she could actually choose something healthy that she really wanted. That's our ideal outcome anyway. Unfortunately, even without the burden of reenactment, we don't always seem to make healthy choices - have you noticed that? In the next chapter, we'll take a look at possible reasons why.

CHAPTER 19

Why Do We Struggle?

Way back in the early 1940s, Abraham Maslow introduced his 'hierarchy of needs' and the idea that all humans share an actual *need* for self-actualization. This, though, was the very top of the pyramid. The idea is that once our more basic needs are met, we're free to pursue our true potential as individuals, to move into the 'zone of genius', as author Gay Hendricks puts it, where we're living our most authentic life and truly contributing something to the world that's unique to us.

How does that sound?

Probably not all that interesting if you're totally starving right now. That growling stomach is pretty distracting! What you really want out of life might just be a sandwich. Or maybe you just got kicked out and need to find a new place to live *pronto*. Well, put down this book and go check Craigslist again!

Clearly, Maslow put self-actualization at the top of the pyramid for good reason. If we're thirsty, or feel unsafe, or don't have any friends or a sweetheart, or we're working at a crummy dead-end job and barely scraping by, that makes it tough to dream big – which is what *I'd* like you to do.

Why Are So Many People Struggling?

Near the end of his life, Maslow wondered why more people weren't self-actualizing. Most of us are living in times of unprecedented prosperity, at least in the Western world. Wouldn't you think folks would have their basic needs squared away? What keeps people from becoming their highest and best selves?

At the risk of seeming totally paranoid, I think you've been seriously messed with. I think we all have. Some of this is inadvertent – just growing up in a family. And some of it seems quite deliberate, and this is the paranoid bit. I believe that it benefits those in power if you are stuck on the lower rungs of Maslow's pyramid, which makes you easier to manage and keeps you consuming goods and services at a much higher rate. See, I told you I was paranoid. But let's do take a look at some of the influences that keep us on those lower rungs of the pyramid, starting with the family.

Our Family

We're all born with a powerful biological imperative to fit into our family. No matter how crazy it is, we have to figure out our place in the family system, and the more dysfunctional our parents are, the more likely we are to get stuck in an unhealthy role. Here are some of the classics:

The Enabler –the child is '*parentified*' and steps in to pick up the slack for a Mom or Dad who just can't seem to cope.

The Clown – this child is given the job of diffusing tension and bringing everyone together while still avoiding difficult issues.

The Hero – this child brings honor to the family through her achievements, but has a desperate need to be perfect.

The Black Sheep – this one just can't do anything right, such a disappointment! She brings the family together when they try to 'fix' her, and helps the Hero shine brighter by contrast.

The Little Doll – this child has the job of making a narcissistic parent look good through superficial appearance and manners.

The Lost Child – this one takes up as little space as possible and tries to be invisible.

Are any of these familiar to you? Being stuck in any kind of role is definitely going to make self-awareness more difficult. Even the injunction to be a good person really means following a set of rules written by somebody else. You weren't put here on Earth to be 'good'. You're here to be you – a job that no one else can do.

Many families have unspoken rules that can be seriously limiting. It's not okay to make more money than Dad. You can't be slim when Mom struggled with weight her whole life. How dare you try to follow your dream when Dad had to sacrifice his own dream just to put food on the table? Or how about, "All the men in this family are physicians – music is a hobby, not a career."

Familial roles and expectations can make it hard to even *admit* your ambition, let alone pursue it. It feels selfish somehow and may even trigger fears of being abandoned. Getting clear on any conflicts between what you really want and what was okay in your family of origin can be crucial. Luckily, all of these conflicts can be tapped on with EFT.

Advertising

I'm sure you're aware there's an *enormous* advertising industry with extremely clever people working day and night to influence what you think you want and who you think you are. And they're *very* good at what they do.

Advertisers understand very clearly what people truly want and need to feel secure and happy. They know all about Maslow's pyramid and have it all down to a science. Whatever they're selling is *the* solution for that problem they're making you so painfully aware of.
Want to experience intimacy? You need whiter teeth and fresher breath!
Want to be admired (or better yet, envied)? A new car is the answer! Or that designer bag you're seeing everywhere! Or a Rolex will do the trick!
Want to fit in? This season all the cool kids are wearing Hush Puppies!
Not sexy enough? Botox! Implants! Eyelash extensions!

People want a sense of connection with others. We want to feel included, seen, loved and appreciated. And perhaps desired. We want to feel special, unique. And that we're winning. We want to be 'in the know'. If we think a product can do this for us, we're sold!

The advertising industry does *not* have your best interests at heart. They'll shatter your self-esteem just to pick your pocket. Seriously. The more worthless we feel, the greater our need to compensate, to somehow feel superior. And the more we're willing to spend.

Advertising is designed to keep us feeling unimportant, insecure, unattractive, scared of missing out, anxious about life, and ideally, hovering just above despair.

So, when you ask yourself, "What do I want?" it's a good idea to check for implants from the industry. Do you really want a 'Coke and a smile'? Or just the smile? Do you really want that bikini? Or do you want to love your body and feel attractive?

Cultural Conditioning

Along with the Pepsi and iPhones, we've been sold a carefully engineered version of reality – one that harnesses and exploits our reality generating powers in service of someone else's agenda.

From the time we're little, we're conditioned to accept our culture and society as natural and inevitable. We adopt a set of expectations for how life can be and *should* be, of human nature, what money is, how disease and healing work, what love is and what we can hope for. We accept a social order and political power structure as just the way things are.

Why is this relevant? It's been said that fish aren't aware of the water they swim in. In many ways, we're just as immersed in an unseen cultural medium, but unlike the fish, we're drowning in it. To some extent, this is the 'reality' we're hacking. Stepping out of it might be a shock at first, but ultimately a real breath of fresh air.

Let's look at two more of the *biggest* cultural programmers. These are major players: school and the media, both very intentional and successful forms of cultural programming.

Schooling

Okay, before we dive in, please don't get the idea that I'm criticizing teachers. Many of the best people I know are teachers – dedicated, creative and astonishingly hard working. But let's take a look at the system itself.

For the past 150 years, compulsory public schooling has played a huge role in social conditioning. Wealthy industrialists like Rockefeller and Carnegie set up the US school system, importing techniques designed by the Prussians. It was deliberately engineered to produce docile factory workers, obedient civil servants, and soldiers who would follow orders without question. Intellectual curiosity and critical thinking skills were suppressed in favor of unquestioning acceptance of authority.

Short study periods ending with loud buzzers or ringing bells would interrupt and thus frustrate a child's natural interest and curiosity. Learning was broken up into small, discreet subjects to discourage big picture thinking. A focus on memorization and regurgitating the 'correct' answer replaced open-ended discussion.

The elites who established public education didn't send their own children to these schools. They still don't.

By removing children from home at a young age, schooling sought to diminish or break the influence of the family, replacing it with fealty to the State. Segregating children by age was another divisive tactic, further weakening bonds between siblings and increasing reliance on the one adult available. Most of us probably take it for granted, but schools are the only place this kind of age segregation ever happens. It's pretty weird when you think about it.

Schools grade children much as we grade meat and eggs, another bizarre idea we generally accept without questioning. Instead of helping each child develop their native talents, interests, and aptitudes, they're sorted into winners and losers for the convenience of prospective employers.

Perhaps the most insidious idea here is that children only learn when they're forced to. They have to go to a special building, removed from the normal life of their community, and undergo an artificial system of rewards and punishments to motivate them. Left to their own devices, children would grow up to be ignorant, illiterate morons. Ironically literacy rates have steadily fallen since the advent of compulsory schooling – as was intended!

I hope you had a *wonderful* time in school. But even if all of your teachers were excellent, and all of your classmates charming, 12+ years of conditioning may have imposed unnecessary and unhelpful limitations on how you see yourself and the world and what you imagine is available to you now. It's good to know this because it's totally possible to tap those limitations away!

The Media

We watch *programs*. And yes, we're programmed by them. We're fed a steady stream of ideas, beliefs, moral constructs and political narratives embedded in the plot, dialogue, and context of each show. The same is true whether we're watching a sitcom or the news. Choose your flavor – Fox News or NPR, it's really the same programming.

Because there's so much *apparent* diversity of choice, and because we're *choosing* to watch or listen, we tend to let our guard down, soaking it all up with little or no critical resistance. It's human nature to want to trust and like the people on our screens. All too often we're like children in their hypnogogic state.

At the time of this writing nearly every channel of the media – television and movies, newspapers and magazines, popular music and talk radio, top blogs, and social media content – is owned and controlled by five or six corporations! Which themselves are owned and controlled by a few powerful dynastic families. Really just a few thousand people.

Do these folks have an agenda for us? And does the content of their programming reflect their agenda? What do you think? The owners of these multi-billion-dollar media empires are also stakeholders in other huge sectors of the economy, including agribusiness, fossil fuels, pharmaceuticals, defense contracting, health care, the prison-industrial sector, and finance, to name a few.

Each one of these sectors has become increasingly vertically integrated, parasitical and destructive, even deadly. Public awareness and attitudes are carefully managed to promote unthinking acceptance of *that's just the way it is*. We're kept in a state of perpetual fear, anxiety, and not-enoughness – the lower rungs of Maslow's pyramid.

We're intended to fit into the existing system, not change it. Our self-actualization is not part of the plan.

Most grocery stores in the US have banks of glossy magazines in the checkout isles. Mostly targeting women, they promise solutions to *urgent* problems – keep your man happy, keep him interested in bed, lose those extra pounds, stay young looking, give your kids the competitive edge they'll need, get that bikini body in time for summer.

Keeping women insecure, obsessed with trivial concerns, disempowered and feeling bad about themselves (especially compared to the glamorous celebrities on the cover) is certainly done to sell them stuff. No question. But it also keeps women distracted and thus disinterested in challenging the status quo – women who might otherwise be fierce protectors of their children's future on Earth. Just sayin'.

Asked "What would you like?" how many women might automatically say, "I want to lose 15 pounds?" And that's fine. I don't mean to be critical. But if that desire wasn't essentially *implanted*, along with a sense of shame and urgency, what might the answer be otherwise? Might there be a deeper, more authentic answer?

Whenever I work with a new client suffering from intense anxiety, I always ask them to go on a media fast - or at least to avoid 'the news'. This might be good advice for all of us, to take a break from the onslaught of what's wrong with the world at large and with ourselves. If you find it difficult to take a few days off that might be a sign you should take a few *weeks* off!

Questions to Ask Yourself

To tune into what it is that would genuinely help you reach a state of self-actualization, and to be living from your 'zone of genius', think about these questions:

What makes me feel most alive, excited, turned on, energized and happy?

If money wasn't a concern, what would I most like to do or explore?

Are there interests I've pushed away because they seem trivial or selfish?

Have I ever had a 'peak experience'? What was it all about?
Given the freedom, what would I most like to do with the rest of my life?

It's vital to know what you want out of life, but sometimes that's pretty much the opposite of what you're experiencing. In our next chapter, we'll look into why that might be.

CHAPTER 20

Reverse Engineering

D o you have a list of goals right now? If not, you should probably put this book down and go make one right now. But please come back when you're finished!

Goals are kind of trippy. They can be short-term, long-term, concrete or abstract, modest or totally over the top. Whether they're about career, relationships, health, hygiene, travel, spirituality, wealth or whatever, our goals set an intention to make our life better. Without at least some destination in mind, we're liable to just drift along. And maybe that's okay, in a kind of Zen-hippy live for the moment sort of way.

Then again, lack of direction makes us more vulnerable to living out someone else's plan for our life, which definitely sucks.

Sometimes we may be saddled with a negative kind of plan we came up with all by ourselves in childhood. There was someone we despised so much that we made a vow to never be like them – and now we're stuck living out the opposite extreme. If that person was selfish, we're giving to a fault. If they were pushy, we're a human doormat. If they were arrogant, we're self-effacing to the point of dysfunction.

I've had many clients who were trapped in this kind of polarity. Alas, 180 degrees from dysfunction is equal and opposite dysfunction. To reach the healthy middle ground, I ask them to take just a few tiny steps in the direction of that person they were so disgusted by. To take just one tiny homeopathic dose of that selfishness or arrogance that's so distasteful.

Competing Wish Lists

Perhaps you've noticed, even when you have clearly defined goals, things don't always turn out the way you'd like. You might be pursuing a goal with clear intentions, careful planning, positive energy and lots of hard work – and things *still* don't work out. In fact, you might even manifest the opposite! Why is that?

Whatever goals we pursue, whatever accomplishments, possessions, and experiences we seek, what we're *really* after are the feelings we think those things will bring us. And of course, that's always some flavor of happy – excitement, security, sensual pleasure, a sense of accomplishment or satisfaction, the joy of self-expression, making one's parents proud, the warm glow of virtue, or even darker pleasures like pride, superiority, or inspiring envy in others.

One common problem here is that we may be totally wrong – the thing we *think* will give us that feeling won't. The Universe knows better. It knows what we're really after and sends us off on what seems to be a totally frustrating tangent. This often becomes clear in hindsight, but while it's happening, to the extent we're attached to what we think we want, we're liable to suffer.

Another and perhaps bigger problem is that your subconscious has its own wish list and it's all about survival. Things like happiness and satisfaction don't even register. All those wonderful feelings from achieving your goals? Not a priority for your subconscious mind. To the contrary. Those goals are all about changing your life, right? Well, your subconscious has a pretty strong anti-change agenda.

You're still alive right? So *something* must be working. So the subconscious says, 'Hey, let's just keep doing exactly the same thing that's gotten us this far'. Or at least it would be saying that if there was any sort of conscious intelligence there. There's not.

Whenever you're stymied, and especially when the same unwanted thing keeps happening over and over again despite your best efforts, that's a pretty clear sign that your subconscious has added a few items to your wish list, up near the top, written with invisible ink. *Your* goals have been eclipsed.

In this sense, what we call 'self-sabotage' is really self-protection. We're being protected from our own 'crazy' attempts to change our life by the oppressive inertia of our subconscious mind.

So your current goal of being a successful artist conflicts with that childhood decision to always be invisible. Or you want to be a rich and successful CEO, but your subconscious *knows* that will make you a target - it's not safe! You say you'd like to lose 40 pounds? That's crazy! Don't you remember? Being thin means unwanted attention from men. Your subconscious remembers.

When there's a conflict like that, guess who tends to win? We might push through for a while with will power and discipline, but sooner or later we get tired and then watch out.

The Hidden Agenda

This whole 'let's keep everything the same' agenda pretty much sucks, but it gets worse. A lot worse. One of the top priorities for the subconscious is to discharge the Freeze Response and get those 'trauma capsules' out of our system. That doesn't sound too bad, right?

It wouldn't be bad at all if we were like other mammals. We'd just have to shake like the impala, discharging all of the pent up energy in our muscles that got trapped when Flight got interrupted. That shaking is simply repeating or reenacting the muscular motions of Flight, and repetition is the *only* thing the subconscious knows how to do. This works well for the impala, actually increasing its resilience.

But our *human* Fight or Flight is rarely triggered by some critter trying to run us down and eat us. For us, it's all about social situations. I'm 2 years old, and mom is yelling at me, or I'm 7, and all the kids at school are laughing at me, or I'm 12, and mom and dad are divorcing. *That's* what's going to be repeated for us. Instead of just shaking it off, we get to endure a series of social reenactments.

And the subconscious is *extremely* good at setting up these reenactments for us. It's tied into the quantum field and collective unconscious and somehow pulls people into your life to replay key roles – the person who cheats on you, or bullies you, or desperately needs you to save them. Somehow it can arrange all sorts of events for you to replay – from getting laid off to being rear-ended at a stoplight.

There's no creative intelligence behind this, it really is just repetition. But it *seems* like the big idea is that maybe this time things will work out. Maybe this time you'll get it right. Maybe this time you'll stand up for yourself. Maybe this time Dad will listen to you instead of yelling. Maybe this time you'll be able to get away or fight back. Maybe this time you'll finally be appreciated.

Only it never seems to work out that way. Instead of resolution, the feelings and beliefs just get reinforced. Repetition creates ever stronger morphic fields. Remember that old definition of crazy? Doing the same thing over and over again and expecting different results? Reenactment sucks!

Your subconscious wants those trauma capsules gone. To be fair, that really is a good idea. Those capsules are very much like cysts in the psyche. They contain dangerous emotional intensity, and there's always a risk of them leaking or rupturing. Also, it takes a lot of energy to contain them and keep them all sealed up with dissociation. They really do need to be resolved, just not through reenactment.

Shutting it Down

Reverse engineering means working backwards to figure something out. As crazy as it might seem, if the same sort of bad thing keeps happening over and over, let's assume some part of us actually *wants* that bad experience or somehow wants us to feel those terrible feelings again. In that case, who or what is this reenactment all about?

Helpful questions to ask might be:

What does this experience remind you of?
Have you ever felt this way before? If so, when was the first time?
If your horrible boss (or whoever) was 'standing in' for someone from childhood, who would that person be?

We're playing a game of 'Connect the dots' here, where each dot is some terrible but similar experience. What event is your subconscious mind trying to resolve? Almost always the first 'dot' is one of your younger selves, six years old or younger, trapped in a bad memory, endlessly reliving it like a tape loop from hell. Keep in mind, even small events can have a huge emotional impact on a little child.

And that emotional impact or distress is the driving force behind the whole dynamic of reenactment. Those feelings are *intolerable* for the psyche and the subconscious imperative to resolve them (through reenactment) can easily outweigh your current hopes, dreams, goals, and ambitions.

It's important to realize that your younger selves aren't aware of you. They don't know you exist. They aren't out to get you! Even if they're wreaking total havoc in your life today, *they are not your enemy*. It might be easy to hate them but don't. It's crucial to adopt a compassionate attitude toward them – to give them the love and support you'd give any other child.

Possession

Anytime our behavior is compulsive and self-destructive, we can feel almost possessed as if there's some kind of demon inside. This is a belief promoted by certain religions and one that's easily adopted by those who've been cut off from their younger selves by intense shame and self-hatred.

I don't believe in actual demons and consider the notion totally unhelpful. It's an idea that exacerbates a sense of powerlessness and victimization. In my experience, there's *always* a younger self at the root and they really just need our help.

I'm not saying that compulsive behavior isn't scary. I've watched my own hand bringing cake toward my mouth when I'm already feeling stuffed and don't want anymore. It's quite alarming – who the hell has control of my hand?! The more cut off we are by dissociation, the freakier our encounters with a younger self.

Rescue Mission

Reverse engineering means finding the younger selves at the root of your issues, and then the real work of tapping them out of the Freeze Response begins. There are really two ways to go about it. With basic EFT you can allow the feelings of your younger self to come into your body now and tap away the intensity. This might be enough to free them and shut down the pattern of reenactment.

The second and deeper level of healing is entering into their scene through Matrix Reimprinting, tapping on the younger self directly and helping them achieve a new and better picture to reimprint. This goes beyond removing the emotional distress by reversing whatever negative decisions they made at the time. It can be harder to pull this off on our own (it's usually best to work with a Matrix practitioner) but still totally worth a try.

It usually takes more than helping one or two younger selves, but eventually, we cross a tipping point. Then the weight loss becomes effortless. The bullies go away. Your new partner would never dream of cheating on you. You finally get to start having what *you* wrote on that wish list.

How does that sound? If we're going to succeed in this mission, we'll need some tools, and the greatest of them all is EFT tapping. The next section begins with our crash course in EFT and how to make it really work wonders. We'll then explore some surprising ways it can be leveraged for huge life changes. Stay tuned!

Part II

TOOLS FOR TRANSFORMATION: THE WAYS AND MEANS OF MIRACULOUS CHANGE

"There are only two ways to live your life. One is as though nothing is a miracle. The other is as though everything is a miracle."
--- Albert Einstein

CHAPTER 21

EFT Crash Course

Are you ready to learn our primary hacking tool? The 'basic recipe' for EFT Tapping is so easy children can learn to do it. At the same time, there's really no limit to how deep you can go with this amazing healing modality.

Below are simple written instructions along with a tapping points chart you can download. There's also a link to a helpful how-to video. If you've never experienced EFT, don't worry about getting it right, just muddle through as best you can. You may be surprised at how well it works right out of the gate!

The Basic Recipe

Here is EFT in five simple steps. We'll look at each of these in more detail below:

1. State the problem (be as specific as you can).

2. Rate how distressing the problem is right now from zero to ten.

3. Do a 'set-up statement' by tapping on the side of your hand and saying: "Even though I have this problem (whatever it is), I deeply love and completely accept myself."

4. Tap around all the points while stating this problem for each point. Go around again and again until you start to feel better.

5. Re-measure the intensity from zero to ten. Repeat steps 3-5 until the intensity is at a zero.

EFT Tapping Points

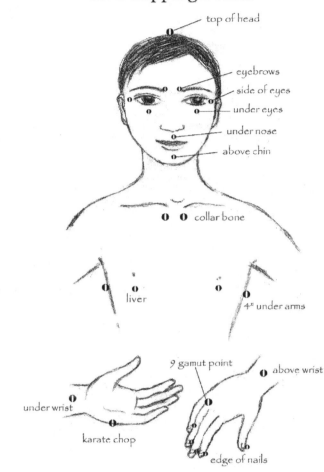

To download and print this image, and watch my how-to video click here: tappingthematrix.com/free-how-to-tap-resources/

Tapping in Detail

Step 1. State the problem

This is the most important step to get right, which means being as specific as possible. Maybe you're feeling crummy and decide to tap. You could go ahead and tap on "Even though I feel so crummy, I deeply love and completely accept myself." But what does 'crummy' actually mean?

It might include being a little sick to your stomach, some anxiety about an upcoming work meeting, feeling resentful that your partner didn't do the dishes last night, and a twinge of guilt because you still haven't called your mom back and it's been five days.

So 'crummy' is really a big tangled ball of yuck. To be most effective with EFT it's best to tap on one strand at a time. You might do the basic recipe for each thing, and do them one at a time. Or, you could do the whole mess, but make sure and name each strand as you tap through the points.

If you're tapping on a distressing memory, what are the key parts of what happened? And what feelings are coming up? Be sure to tap on all the specific parts.

Step 2. Rate the intensity

Our zero to ten scale is often called the 'SUD Level.' SUD stands for Subjective Units of Distress (or Discomfort if it's a physical issue). Don't worry about being super accurate with the numbers. Just a guess is good enough.

If you're tapping on an old memory, rate the intensity you're feeling now, not at the time it happened.

With EFT things can change pretty fast. If the intensity *isn't* going down, or only very slowly, there's a good chance what you're tapping on isn't specific enough, and specific really refers to what's wrong right now at this moment.

Step 3. The Set Up Statement

Tap on the side of your hand below the pinky – this is often called the 'Karate Chop Point.' It doesn't matter which hand you tap on.

The Set Up Statement activates our specific issue in the limbic brain so that the effects of the tapping are targeted. It also lowers resistance to change, at least temporarily. And finally, it balances out the problem with a key affirmation:

"Even though I have this _____, I deeply love and completely accept myself" or
"Even though I have this _____, I chose to forgive myself, as best I can" or
"Even though I have this _____, I want to get to a calm and peaceful place."

Just fill in the _____ with whatever specific problem you'd like to change.

Notice we're saying "I have this anger" instead of saying, "I am angry", or whatever the problem is. It isn't crucial to use this language, but it's helpful. We acknowledge the problem without identifying with it.

I suggest doing the Set Up Statement just once per round of tapping.

Step 4. Tap through the points

Tap on each point, starting at the top of the head and working your way down your body. We usually tap about 7-10 times on each point, though the exact number isn't important. With each point say a 'reminder phrase' to keep the problem activated.

You can simply repeat the same words over and over: "This headache, this headache, this headache, this headache..." but after a while, the repetition gets a bit boring, and the words might start to lose their meaning. Better to use descriptive adjectives to hone in even *more* specifically.

So, you might say, "This headache, this headache on the right side of my head, this splitting headache, this sharp pain when I move my head too fast, this sharp stabbing pain on the right side of my head,

this headache, this frustrating headache that just won't go away...."
And so on.

You don't need a PhD in psychology to know what words to say. Simply describe every aspect of what's wrong as you tap along. Even if you do just say the same words over and over, it's still likely to help quite a bit.

You'll notice that some points are on the midline, while others are bilateral. It really doesn't matter whether you tap on both sides or just one or the other, though if I have both hands free, I'll usually tap on both sides just because it feels better.

The less you actually think about the act of tapping the better. Ideally, you're focused on the problem at hand. There's no need to stop once you've gone through all the points. More often we'll go around and around the points in 'rounds' until noticing a shift in how we feel.

Step 5. Re-measure the intensity

Our scale in EFT is zero to ten, and that zero is important. Zero means the problem (or our emotional intensity *about* the problem) is totally gone, which suggests that it's much less likely to come back. Ideally, we always try to tap the issue down to zero.

Sometimes there can be a 'better quit while we're ahead' kind of feeling. If the SUD level drops from 8 to a 3, that feels pretty amazing! So let's not push our luck, right? No! Keep tapping! Get that intensity as close to zero as you can.

Focusing on the Negative

Remember my advice to be specific in Step One? That really means be specific about what's wrong. EFT is all about discharging and sloughing off the old, negative, worn out stuff that doesn't belong, which means we really need to name it! This can be disconcerting, especially for Law of Attraction devotees. There's a superstition that saying anything negative will attract it *to* us. Don't worry! It doesn't work that way with tapping.

If a negative thought isn't already stuck in your subconscious, I guarantee you won't implant it with EFT. The words will just go in one ear and out the other.

On the other hand, if we name something negative that *is* lurking in the subconscious, there's often a little spike in emotional intensity as it's discharged. Even if there's a *big* spike in intensity, it's always followed by immediate relief – kind of like throwing up after eating something spoiled. You feel *so* much better once it's out of your system.

Cleaning Out the Wound

Imagine you fell and got a gash in your arm, all full of dirt and grime and little bits of gravel. You go to the ER, and a nurse says, "Oh my! That looks pretty bad. Let's get that all wrapped up in some nice sterile bandages."

You might be worried that she skipped a step – and rightly so! Unless she thoroughly cleans out the wound and gets all of that crud out of it, how can it heal? It's way more likely to get infected.

EFT is all about cleaning out the wounds so they can finally heal. Don't be afraid to name, acknowledge and *feel into* the worst of it while tapping. In my workshops, I've coined the phrase, "Go for the jugular!"

That said, it's totally okay to tap on positive statements. There's value in affirming that we love, accept and forgive ourselves. It can be helpful to voice the way we'd *like* things to change and tap into gratitude. Just don't shy away from clearing out the scary bad stuff too.

A Simple Trick

When you do tap on your own, I highly recommend using a timer. If your mind is anything like mine, it's a slippery devil. I'll start tapping on an issue and suddenly realize I'm looking at Facebook or doing the dishes. How did *that* happen?

These days I just set a timer and keep tapping until it dings. I recommend doing 5 to 8 minutes at a go. Maybe 12 minutes for really difficult issues. Then check the SUD level and do a second round if need be. I've been doing this timer trick for the last few years, and it's made a huge difference for me.

Working with a Practitioner

EFT is a fantastic self-help tool, but sometimes it's best to work with an experienced practitioner. If you're dealing with severe abuse memories, heavy depression, panic attacks or anything really overwhelming, it's best to get some expert help. Especially if you're feeling fragile or freaked out. Even with 'garden variety' life issues, you'll likely make more progress working with someone good. But don't wait! Have at it on your own!

Take it for a Spin

Are you ready to take EFT for a test drive? Pick an issue you'd like to see change. Go through those 5 simple steps and have a go! Or if you'd like to watch my how-to video first, here's the link again:

tappingthematrix.com/free-how-to-tap-resources/

Now that you've got this crash course under your belt, let's explore one very powerful way to really supercharge your EFT results.

CHAPTER 22

Going for the Jugular

O ne of the quickest ways to dissolve our fears is to simply acknowledge them while tapping. This is why with EFT we want to focus on the negative. Tapping brings the shadow of our fears into the light of awareness, allowing them to gently melt away.

Fear is supposed to help keep us safe. That's its job. And happily, we can't tap away what's supposed to be there. We can't override healthy caution with EFT – tapping on fear of heights won't lead us to step off of a tall building.

For most of us though, we have way too much fear. It's not actually helpful. Even if we're facing a genuinely dire situation, fear takes blood away from our frontal cortex which makes it harder to think clearly. We're more apt to be jumpy, to react rather than respond to situations. Fear is generally counterproductive.

And often we're not even in dire circumstances. We can become totally obsessed with something terrible that *might* happen. This can really diminish our quality of life!

"Even If" Tapping

My students tend to be really nice people. One of the few real challenges I face teaching EFT is helping them come to grips with this focus on the dark side. We all want to help people feel better, and here I am asking them to basically rub their client's nose in whatever's wrong. It just feels so counterintuitive.

But it also works wonders.

'Going for the jugular' means tackling the very worst of what's wrong. The darkest fears. The worst-case scenario. It's one of the best ways with EFT to leverage massive, profound, life-changing improvements.

Normally with EFT, we begin our set-up statements with "Even though...." We tack on whatever memory, feeling, or current situation is upsetting us and finish up with an affirmation. Recently I've been using a simple variant to accommodate 'going for the jugular." I call it *'Even if* tapping.

The idea here is to really *go for it*. Acknowledge and verbalize the really scary stuff. Whatever we're most afraid of. It really would be cruel doing this, if it weren't for the magic of tapping. Here are a few examples:

"Even if the test results come back positive, and I'm given just a few months to live and end up dying young, without ever really accomplishing what I wanted to do in this life... I still want to get to a calm and peaceful place and fully enjoy whatever time I have left."

"Even if we actually *do* get divorced, and I lose her and her family and most of our friends forever and never find anyone new and end up alone for the rest of my life... I still want to feel good about myself and my life."

"Even if my company totally goes under and I lose my job and can't get hired again anywhere because I'm too old and the economy is shit, *and* I totally blow through all my savings and end up deep into debt just trying to get by and end up destitute and homeless... I still choose to relax as best I can and choose to see my life as a success."

"Even if I never meet my soul mate and never do have children, and my eggs just dry up and blow away and I'm single for the rest of my life and never have the wonderful family I've always dreamed about, and disappoint my parents and feel empty and unfulfilled for the rest of my life... I still deeply love and completely accept myself."

This can be really edgy stuff. If you're new to tapping, you might not want to start with this level of intensity. It takes guts to go there, to name your absolute worst fears and really trust the tapping to work its magic.

But that magic means fear loses its hold on you. From a Law of Attraction standpoint, your fears become far less likely to ever manifest when they lose their emotional charge. You become free to explore much more positive territory and create a better future.

Stirring the Pot

Whenever I'm 'going for the jugular' with a client, there's a genuine risk I might introduce a new fear that hadn't occurred to them before. That sucks! Luckily it doesn't happen often, because theoretically I might make them feel even worse – and I take that "First, do no harm" idea seriously. In practice though, it never seems to work that way.

Even if I brought up something they hadn't thought of yet, the key word there is 'yet'. And now, after the briefest moment of distress, the fear is neutralized by our tapping, and they're essentially immune to it. The relief that follows is very often accompanied by laughter!

Laughter is one of the most wonderful signs that EFT is working. Our deeply buried fears are apt to grow all out of proportion. They *feel* terrifying but brought up into the light of awareness they're often ludicrous. Recognition of their absurdity, along with the sweet relief this brings, can make us literally laugh out loud.

A really good practitioner should be able to help you explore and release your deepest darkest fears. It's not as easy to do this on your own, but there *is* a way, and I'm happy to share it with you here.

Writing Your Own Script

Gary Craig, the founder of EFT, has always regarded tap-along videos and scripts as the lowest form of tapping. I have to agree with him because by nature they're a generic, one size fits all approach, which is inherently less effective.

But that all changes when you write your *own* script. That can make it a very powerful tool indeed.

Anytime you're facing a bad situation, intractable problem or distressing emotions, you can sit down and type out a simple set up statement and then line after line of everything that's wrong. This is where you really 'go for the jugular.' It can be pretty intense doing this. In fact, it *should* be intense if you're really getting to the core of what's upsetting you.

Once you've got it all typed out, it's time to start tapping. Just tap and tap and tap as you read through your script, and then start over from the top. Tap until you feel a shift.

If your issue is a really big deal, consider tapping through your script several times a day. It might take days and days, or even weeks to get to a calm and peaceful, neutral sort of place with it. But you will.

After a while, certain lines in your script, certain specific aspects of the issue, will probably start losing their emotional intensity. Just delete those lines and carry on. Then again, you may have new ones show up as you get deeper into it – no worries! This is actually a good thing. Just add the new material to your script and keep tapping.

Eventually, the issue or emotions that were plaguing you will begin to fade away. You'll probably lose interest in doing the tapping once the intensity drops below a certain threshold. Try to stick with it though, until all the charge is gone. Just keep deleting whatever lines become neutral until the whole damn thing is down to zero.

Speaking from personal experience, it can take a bit of courage to do this, but going after the darkest, scariest 'even if' stuff has brought about the sweetest miracles.

On the Other Hand...

Now that I've touted the virtues of staying negative while tapping let me just add - there's definitely room for positive statements too, especially as you come to a close. I make such a big deal about staying with the negative simply because most people really are uncomfortable with it. Without addressing what's wrong, our tapping is relatively worthless, but there's ample room for balancing out the negative stuff while tapping. You'll notice in the script below that I *do* end on a positive note.

And speaking of positive notes, in the next chapter we'll explore the weird and paradoxical idea that no matter what's wrong, maybe *nothing* is wrong - that's pretty damn positive, right? But first, here's a nice 'going for the jugular' kind of sample script to check out.

A Sample Script for Negative Expectations

Tapping on the karate chop point:
Even though I'm not really expecting anything good to happen, and honestly I'm just waiting for the next blow, I forgive myself for that.

Tapping around the points:
I'm so sick of living this way
I feel so hopeless
nothing good is going to happen
nothing that lasts anyway
every good thing just gets taken away
it's just going to hurt when that happens
the happier I let myself feel, the more it's going to hurt
I know I'm not a bad person
I don't go around hurting other people
but it seems like I really don't deserve love, connection & happiness
at least it doesn't seem to show up very often
or stick around very long
this terrible feeling
there's nothing to look forward to
and really there's nothing I can do to change that
so why bother?
why bother trying so hard?
when it's just going to hurt when it's all taken away from me
no one really loves me
no one really cares about me
no one wants to know who I really am
no one wants to listen
and I know this isn't really true - I do have friends
but it *feels* true

and I've been stuck with this my whole life
these shit-colored glasses
and I forgive myself for that
I've been so sick and so tired and so down for so long
I'm sick and tired of being sick and tired
and it doesn't feel safe to hope for better
I'll just be disappointed
but fuck it
I'm used to disappointment, and I can freaking handle it
I'd like to really lose touch with reality
the reality that says I can't win, I can't be happy, and if I dare to break
the rules I'll pay for it
I give myself permission to notice what's going okay
I give myself permission to notice when I'm feeling better
even if it destroys me
even if it's painful when it's all taken away
I give myself permission to notice when it isn't taken away
when it sticks around
I allow myself to imagine there's light at the end of the tunnel
I forgive myself for being stuck
I forgive myself for anything I've done to become so ill
I forgive myself for feeling hopeless
I love myself for wanting a better life even when it feels hopeless

CHAPTER 23

The Paradox of Helping

Imagine you're standing on the deck of a ship and suddenly hear a splash. Someone has fallen overboard! They're totally struggling, maybe drowning! What do you do?

Your first impulse might be to leap in and try to save them. I salute your altruism, but then again, even if you're a very strong swimmer, you might just end up drowning with them. Misery loves company and all, but that's not all that helpful, really.

So on second thought, maybe there's a life preserver hanging on the wall nearby – the kind with a long rope attached. Might be worth a quick look around! Staying put on deck has the possible benefit of actually saving them. Not to mention *you* not drowning.

Whenever we're trying to help someone who is truly suffering, this is basically our dilemma. Our own empathy can have us right in there, drowning with them – which absolutely reduces our helpfulness. But how can we reach them and still keep at least one foot on solid ground?

Terra Firma

There's a seeming paradox at the heart of the issue of helping that I've had to wrestle with in attempting to become an effective healer. On one hand, I'm keenly aware of my client's suffering. I know it's absolutely real for them. Perhaps the most 'real' thing in their life at the moment.

At the same time, my spiritual perspective suggests that actually, only a small part of my client is suffering, and almost always that suffering is based on a narrow, limited and fear-based belief about who they are and how life is. I know that their true self, their Soul, is magnificent beyond comprehension and the Sufferer is only a tiny part of themselves crammed into a distorted personality structure.

To put it another way, the suffering is real, but the sufferer is not.

For me, keeping one foot firmly planted in both realities, the material and the spiritual, enables me to do my best work. Embracing this apparent paradox is my way of standing on solid ground while helping someone drowning in deep water. Total empathy in the context of a dispassionate perspective. It can be quite a stretch sometimes.

When I do manage it though, it's less like tossing my client a life ring and more like simply taking their hand while the waves melt away, and somehow, we're standing in a lovely sunlit garden that was there all the time. That's on a good day.

I think it's possible to accomplish this, even with the most turbulent crisis or godawful trauma, because the garden is a lot more *real* than the waves. The waves are surprisingly optional, basically determined by our perceptual filters.

Don't Just Do Something, Stand There!

In the last year or so I've been playing with a new idea that's so basic, so simple, it seems almost too easy. The idea is that it's much easier to *stop* doing something than it is to start something new.

If you're tired from carrying a heavy burden, it's pretty easy to just set it down or drop it. Especially when you realize it was never yours to carry in the first place. If you're actively doing something to keep success at bay or to prevent your ideal partner from getting anywhere near you, can you see how it might be relatively easy to just stop doing that thing?

There's a seductively logical idea I'd like you to question – if your life isn't all you'd like it to be, if you aren't happy and successful enough, if you have frustrating, intractable problems, the solution is *self-improvement*. Something is missing, something you need to learn, new skills to acquire, new habits to develop. Once you improve yourself enough, you'll finally be able to have what you want.

What if that idea is a dirty trick?

Don't get me wrong. I love learning new stuff and expanding my horizons. It's the *necessity* to do so that I'm questioning. It really comes down to a belief that "Something must change for me to be okay." I'm calling bullshit on that one. You *are* okay, right now, just the way you are, even with all of your problems.

Adapting to Dysfunction

The problem is your mom and dad didn't really want you. Even if they really, really wanted a kid, they probably had some sort of fantasy about what that would be like. They weren't expecting *you*, a real person with real needs.

Even the best parents who are trying so very hard to do it right, they get tired and cross, or just want to use the toilet alone for once. Sooner or later we feel rejected and we always always always blame ourselves. And let's face it, most parents didn't try very hard, and even if they did, they read that damned book by Dr. Spock that told them to leave the baby to cry.

When we're so incredibly helpless, feeling unwelcome or rejected is kind of a big deal. If our real self isn't wanted, we'd better put together a false one. And that's what we do. We put together a false personality based on mistaken beliefs and a whole lot of fear and shame.

Starting as wee children, we cobble together some big, clunky, elaborate apparatus to hide our real selves so we can try to fit in and belong. And it takes a lot of time and energy, work, attention and bother to keep these damned contraptions together. They can be quite rigid, but they're very fragile, really.

Once we allow ourselves to stop, and *let* them fall apart, they actually disintegrate. This can be terrifying! But then we discover our true self that was hidden is magnificent.

The more we can allow our Authentic Self to show up and show through, the more life starts getting really good. The good news is that it's already there! It's been there this whole time. To some extent we really just have to stop whatever we're doing to hide it.

Hide and Seek

Perhaps life on Earth is just one big game of Hide and Seek. We close our eyes, count to 100 and where-oh-where has our Soul gone and hidden now? It's certainly a grand adventure. I deeply believe all of our suffering is meaningful, purposeful, voluntary and temporary. And if the game is getting tiresome, this book is your *Olly Olly Out Are In Free!*

I don't mean to be glib about it. Some folks are living an extremely convincing nightmare. Many of my clients have experienced truly horrific trauma and are still reeling from it. Is it okay to make light of something so dark?

It's definitely a balancing act. Too much empathy and we're right in there drowning with them, and not terribly helpful. Not enough empathy and we're like spiritual sociopaths, saying, "None of this is real anyway, nothing is *really* wrong, so why even bother getting involved?" and turning away.

If you accept the idea that someone's Soul *chose* a traumatic lifetime to learn and grow, then perhaps "why bother getting involved?" is a legitimate question. If they came here to suffer, why not leave 'em to it?

The best answer I've come up with is simply preference. I help people because I want to. Because I enjoy the experience. Because it's satisfying and often a lot of fun. That's good enough for me.

As far as I can tell, from a higher perspective, there's no real obligation to help anyone, and especially no obligation to make a career of it. There are plenty of other perfectly valid things to do here on Earth – creative works and sightseeing come to mind.

I realize this goes against establishment religious imperatives – that we *have* to help others in order to be good. And we'd better be good, or else! But there's a big problem with this orientation.

If my motivation to help others is based on my own need to be a 'good person' then I require their suffering to be real. They must genuinely *need* my help. Otherwise, it doesn't really count. And the more 'real' their problems, the harder it will be to help them. Ugh.

I much prefer it to be easy and fun helping people. I've done enough dismantling of my false personality to know that I'm already a good person (and so are you) with nothing to prove. I'm up for occasional challenges and with no need for 'virtue signaling,' the work can be enjoyable.

Embracing the seeming paradox of helping puts us in a much better position to pull off miracles for ourselves and those around us. Or even those *not* around us, which we'll tackle next.

CHAPTER 24

Working with Others in the Matrix

Have you ever seen a film where someone is trying to jump a freight train? It's just starting to roll out of the yard, and they have to run like hell to catch up and match the speed of the train. There's that suspenseful little jump as they grab hold of the ladder and swing on up into a boxcar. Once inside they can just sit back and watch the world roll by.

In Matrix Reimprinting we use our imagination to picture the scene we're about to enter. That's our 'running for the train.' Our little jump to get in. But once we do step into that picture, we're no longer relying on imagination, not just making it all up in our head. We're actually there.

This becomes especially clear whenever we're working with someone else in the scene. It might be mom or dad, a sibling perhaps, even the schoolyard bully. Some part of that person actually shows up to work with us. They'll answer our questions honestly and provide needed information. They may be more willing and helpful than normal, but it really is them.

Let me give you an example, but first, a quick mention that while EFT is a fantastic self-help tool, Matrix work is best done with the help of a practitioner.

I Thought There Would Be Blood!

Brigit came to me for help working with her younger self in the womb, just weeks away from being born. The baby seemed to be terrified, and Brigit had no idea why this might be. She'd never heard any stories from her mom or dad that even hinted there'd been a problem.

I had Brigit step into the womb and connect with her younger self there. Sure enough, that baby really *was* in a state of intense fear – but it was her mother's fear she was feeling. The fear hormones surging through mom's bloodstream were coming right through the umbilical cord into the baby's body. And so, the baby was terrified without knowing why.

It didn't take long to tap away the baby's distress. I had Brigit imagine putting a filter on the umbilical cord, to filter out all of mom's distressing neuropeptides. Once the baby was peaceful, I had Brigit step out of the womb and stand next to her pregnant mother, taking her hand.

Mom was standing at her open front door in a state of utter panic. Michael, a former lover, was standing there on the threshold. He'd come unannounced to try and win her back. He hadn't known she was pregnant.

We'd frozen everyone else in the picture, so Michael was standing there like a statue. And luckily so was Brigit's father in the back room. He had a violent temper, and Brigit's mom was certain he would assault or more likely murder her old beau Michael. She was imagining her husband hauled off to prison, leaving her to manage the birth alone and destitute. All of this was flashing through her mind in the moments after opening the door, triggering a tsunami of fear hormones that had swamped the poor little baby inside of her.

We tapped on Mom in the picture, reassuring her that nothing bad would happen at all. Her husband would never learn of the visit, and she'd be fully supported in caring for her new little baby girl. Mom was *intensely* relieved, and it was actually very easy to get rid of Michael – seeing his former lover so very pregnant seemed to collapse his spirit of conquest!

With Michael gone, we were able to reimprint a lovely new picture, helping mom really connect with the baby inside her in a new and more profound way. That lifelong broadcast of fear from the baby was replaced with a new signal of safety and contentment.

But Brigit was intrigued. Her mother had never told her this story. She'd never heard of *any* former lover, let alone a Michael. Had this actually happened? Happily, her mother was still alive and well and happily only a phone call away. Their conversations went something like this:

"Mom, when you were pregnant with me did someone come to the door?"
"Oh heavens! That was Michael! I thought there would be blood! If your father had come out just then; he was so jealous! But...how did you know? I never told anyone about that."

How *did* Brigit know? From my perspective, when we step into a memory in Matrix Reimprinting, we're actually stepping into the event itself as it's stored in the Field. We're usually there to help our own or our client's younger self. But all of the people in that event are available to us.

It's as though they're represented, almost like an icon or image of themselves, but simply by taking their hand and asking questions they're activated in a sense. We open up a connection with them, and at that point, some part of them really does 'show up' to work with us.

Amenable to Change

Sometimes the 'other people' we need to work with were not very nice. Often, they're the ones traumatizing the younger self. The word 'perpetrator' comes to mind. They might be in a rage, or harshly critical, cold and unloving, or even being physically or sexually abusive. You'd think they'd just tell us to piss off, but strangely enough, this rarely happens.

Karl Dawson points out that people in the Matrix are almost *always* more amenable to change than they would have been 'in real life.' And this has been my experience in thousands of sessions.

What are the implications?

This ability to connect with others in the Matrix means we can often do powerful surrogate work for their benefit. We can actually help that person *now*, in real life. And this can also help repair or improve your current relationship with them if that's an issue. This is such a big deal it gets its own chapter – so more on this later.

More often though, the reason we're engaging with 'other' people in the Matrix is to help the younger self we're working with. Their mom, for example, might be being abusive, or neglectful, or somehow causing stress for them. We need mom to knock it off and become more loving, compassionate, forgiving, responsible or kind so the younger self can experience a new, happier reality.

The most powerful way to help mom to change is by tapping to relieve her suffering, allowing her to show up as a much better version of herself. This usually starts off by asking her why she's being so awful – and this is where things often get real for my client. Like Brigit in the story above, they may receive totally new information, or gain new insight into their mom.

When the answers are genuinely surprising, it's obvious that my client couldn't be making it up.

So, if mom, or whoever, really is showing up to work with us, does this actually do anything in the real world? Yes, almost always and sometimes dramatically. I can't tell you how many times I've heard back from a client:

"When I got home the phone rang, and it was my sister! We haven't spoken for seven years."
"I have such a better relationship with my mom now – she's like a different person."
"My dad called up, out of the blue, and apologized to me!"

Money Well Spent

A few years ago, I was in Cambodia touring Angkor Wat. Or at least that was the plan before the dysentery kicked in. I hadn't planned on working but got an emergency email from one of my students. Since I was confined to my room, I went ahead and did a session with her and got a pretty good story out of the deal.

"Emily" had an angry ex. He'd never forgiven her for divorcing him and was once again taking her to court, trying to get 100% custody of their two children. Not because she was a bad mom, and not because he especially cared about the kids. According to Emily he just wanted to mess with her and was trying to get out of paying any child support.

He had plenty of money – enough to keep hiring fancy lawyers. He could easily afford the child support but wanted to punish her. Could we find some way to help him lose his thirst for revenge? The court hearing was scheduled for the next day! Emily wondered if we could do Matrix on one of *his* memories.

He'd told her this story again and again. He was the youngest of six brothers, and they all slept in one bedroom, in three sets of bunk beds. Every night dad would come up the stairs stinking drunk. He'd pull off his belt, choose one of the brothers at random and beat the hell out of him while the brothers watched. As a 5-year-old, her ex was beaten just as often as the others.

Emily was able to picture the scene vividly. I had her imagine stepping into that bedroom to work first with her ex-husband's 5-year-old younger self, and then with his father. Emily had actually met the father a few times, and perhaps this helped her connect with him in the Matrix.

I had her ask him, "Why are you doing this? Why are you beating your own sons?"

He told us this was the only way to make boys into men. It was for their own good. *His* father had beaten *him,* and that's what made a man out of him. Ugh. The great depth psychologist Alice Miller called this 'the poisonous pedagogy,' and it's *so* toxic, adding a layer of self-righteousness to the reenactment of abuse. On top of that, the family was Catholic in Mexico, which added yet another layer of religious sanctimony to the beatings.

Dispelling this pattern meant going back into the dad's childhood to help his younger self. And that meant working with *his* father and even going back to help his father's younger self. I remember we actually tapped on the great grandfather. It was quite a journey, so to speak and really took some doing, but we finally healed that horrible family dynamic.

When we came back to the original scene with that 5-year old we started with, his dad had totally changed – he loved his boys and wouldn't *dream* of beating them. The relief was palpable. But we weren't out of the woods just yet.

With Dad mellowed out, we asked the little 5-year-old (Emily's ex-husband's younger self) what he was feeling. I have to admit I was surprised. That kid wasn't happy at all! Instead, he was very *angry*. Can you guess who he was angry at?

If you guessed Mom, you get a gold star.

This is actually pretty common when one parent is terrifying. It isn't safe to be angry at *them*. For a little kid, it might feel life-threatening. In some families, it might genuinely *be* life-threatening. So the anger is misdirected toward the safest available person, in this case, mom.

The question "Why didn't you protect me?" is legitimate and some of the anger may be entirely valid. But often a whole lot of extra rage gets tacked on – bottled up anger that should really be directed at the abuser. That's what was happening here.

So we brought Mom into the scene and asked her, "Why didn't you protect your son?" She laughed bitterly and said, "Are you joking? I'm being beaten too. This is a living hell for me, but if I run away or if I push him too far and he kills me, then what will become of my children?"

The little 5-year-old took this in wide-eyed and totally forgave his mom on the spot. He suddenly saw that she'd been in a terrible bind, doing the best she could. She could so easily have left to save herself, but she didn't. For the first time, he realized his mom absolutely loved him.

We did some tapping with Mom and let her know that Dad was a changed man now who wouldn't beat her or the boys anymore. Perhaps being a devout Catholic helped her accept what was clearly a miracle!

When we asked the little 5-year-old how he'd like the picture to change, he wanted to do something fun with Mom, just the two of them. I guess being the youngest of six boys can be tough, even in a healthy family. So we sent them off on a lovely picnic, and Emily reimprinted that new picture for the benefit of her ex.

The next day I got an email from Emily. He'd dropped the lawsuit.

Burning Karmic Ribbons

Sometimes the other person we tap on in a picture is no longer living. When we go to the trouble of tapping on them to resolve some traumatic event, my feeling is that we're 'burning karmic ribbons' and this can be profoundly moving. And perhaps now we can skip going through the same sort of drama with them in some other lifetime! No more unfinished business – and that's a wonderful relief!

While we're on the topic of other lifetimes though, can we do this sort of work with our past life selves? Yes, we can! Our very next chapter delves deep into this fascinating subject.

CHAPTER 25

Past Life Resolution

I realize that some people are uncomfortable with the idea of reincarnation. This is one thing hardcore atheists may have in common with the devoutly religious.

No worries! You don't need to believe in past lives to effectively hack your reality, but I will be covering them more in-depth as we go along. If you've been a 'one-lifer', whether, by deliberation or default, I *do* suggest you at least entertain the possibility – if only for practice in stretching the boundaries of your metaphysical 'comfort zone.'

Starving to Death

"Mary" had been battling chronic binge eating her entire adult life. What she described going through sounded pretty intense! Almost like being possessed. Every evening before bed she'd ferociously cram food into her mouth like a savage animal, and couldn't stop until she was physically sick from it.

I had Mary close her eyes, tap gently on her collarbone and ask, "Where did this problem begin for me?" Immediately she saw a young man in a filthy prison cell. Somehow, she knew this was in London and far back in time. He was in chains and literally starving to death. I think it's fair to say we were both astonished that this popped up!

Stepping into that scene, she began tapping on the young man and learned he'd been caught stealing bread. His partner was pregnant and very hungry. Unable to find work, he'd become desperate. He was intensely ashamed of being a thief and for failing his woman and unborn child who would likely die without him.

The life lesson he'd learned from this experience? Hunger is life-threatening and food is scarce and must be stolen and hoarded. These beliefs perfectly matched Mary's binge eating experience, including a kind of furtive sneakiness that had never made any sense to her. She was alone in her own kitchen, so who was she hiding from?

After tapping away his fear, shame, anguish and desperation in the Matrix, we were able to help create a new life picture for this young man – he and his partner were now living on a farm out in the countryside, with honest work and plenty of good nourishing food on hand. The pregnancy was going very well. He now felt a strong sense of honor, dignity, and abundance.

Reimprinting this new picture had a powerful impact on my client and played a major role in ending her binge eating.

Do you believe in past lives? It's one thing to believe in them conceptually. It's quite another thing to experience them personally.

A Passage to India

About 25 years ago I was taking a class where the teachers were doing a past-life regression for each student, one by one, while the rest of us observed. It wasn't my turn that night, I was simply listening to their instructions for my classmate, but all of a sudden, I found myself in a completely different time and place. In fact, *I* seemed to be a different person!

Perhaps because I'm very kinesthetic, I've never been able to visualize very well. So, this sudden experience was unlike anything I'd ever known. I was *there*. And I wasn't just seeing everything; I could smell the spices in the marketplace and feel the oppressive heat. I could feel the packed earth beneath my shoes and hear the cacophony of voices around me.

This was 18th century India. I was an English sailor, apparently stationed in Calcutta long enough that I'd taken an Indian wife and we had a baby daughter. Of course, this was totally against the rules. But we loved each other, and that didn't seem to matter.

Things were probably going pretty well until I got called back to sea. I was forced to leave but promised I'd come back as soon as possible. I left them what money I had, but the final scene of that lifetime shown to me was looking up through beautiful bright green water. I'd fallen overboard and drowned. It was surprisingly peaceful.

But I never returned to my wife and child, and they never found out what became of me. It's likely they thought I'd run off and abandoned them. Life was extremely hard for them after that.

Back in class, the teachers asked the other student, the one who was actually *supposed* to be regressed, to look around and see if anyone in that other lifetime was someone they knew now, in this one. So, of course, I looked too. I saw that my wife and child in that lifetime were my wife and child now. And would it surprise you to learn that we named our little girl India?

It came to me from that experience that one of my main reasons for taking on this current lifetime was to simply take care of my wife and daughter – to balance out that inadvertent abandonment. Talk about some easy karma!

What is Karma Anyway?

Many of our most intense life experiences come in the form of a duality – a relationship with two sides: victim/perpetrator, parent/child, teacher/student, master/slave, caregiver/disabled one, and so on. Often there's a great deal of drama, injustice, suffering and intense emotion bound up in these relationships.

As Souls, we seem drawn to experience both halves of the experience. Perhaps we have an inherent desire for balance and wholeness, but when we've forgotten who we really are and become consumed with guilt, hatred, shame, the desire for revenge, and other really intense emotions, the circular nature of these relationships becomes a spinning wheel that draws us into difficult lifetimes with the same people again and again.

Those of us who've grown up in a Judeo-Christian culture are apt to see karma through the filter of punishment and reward. Bad karma means paying for our sins. Good karma is our reward for virtuous behavior. My problem with this idea is it posits Somebody or Something who is keeping score and serving up just desserts.

As you know by now, I believe *we're* the ones signing up for our lifetimes. I'm sure we receive guidance from our teachers, but there's no angry God meting out punishing lifetimes. I've read that younger Souls do get so caught up in the drama, they sometimes dive right back in without a lot of planning, but it's still up to us. There's no one forcing us to come to Earth and have a terrible time. Whatever mess we find ourselves in, I think it's most helpful to see ourselves as volunteers. And brave volunteers at that.

And that means we always have the choice to step off the spinning wheel of karma. The trick to doing so – the 'cheat code' if you will – is simply love, acceptance and forgiveness. And these are *always* available to each of us in *every* moment. They define our ability to respond to any event or situation.

And our 'ability to respond' is the same thing as 'response ability.' And taking 'responsibility' is not the same as accepting blame. It has nothing to do with guilt or shame. It means actively taking a stance, or adopting an attitude that no matter what is happening, we choose to love and accept ourselves.

This is a kind of purposeful remembering of who we really are. What this life is all about, really. It's seductively easy to see ourselves as victims of circumstance, but we are actually so powerful that once we take responsibility, we can transform not only our own life, but reach back into our past lives as well.

Past lives, really?

Well no, not really. The ones we remember always seem to be in our historical past, to be sure. But remember that quote by Einstein, about time being a persistent illusion? In physics, the only time is now. So our 'past lives' are surely happening now as well. Which is a little hard to get one's head around.

It's also pretty weird that people don't seem to remember 'future lives' set in our own historical future. My guess is that awareness of future lifetimes would violate some sort of basic protocol of earthly reality – remembering them might lead to decisions that would cause them to change or possibly not even happen at all. Very sci-fi! For now, let's stick with the 'past.'

My clients don't seem to remember happy, easy going past lives. On the contrary, there always seems to be something really bad happening. Something that triggered the Freeze Response, no doubt. And this must have created a major wormhole through normal time and space, allowing some really intense and unpleasant feelings to come bleeding through into our current reality.

Let me give you another example.

"Jean" was a gifted healer, but her practice was struggling. She acknowledged a real dread of marketing herself. She didn't even have business cards, much less a website. She'd spent a ton of money on business coaching but could never break through her procrastination. She felt ashamed of her self-sabotage, as she put it.

As we began tapping on this issue, she actually said to me, "I smell smoke." Seriously, I am not making that up! A terrible image came to her – a 'witch' was being burned at the stake. And *she* was that witch.

Scholars today estimate that between 40,000 and 200,000 herbalist, healers and midwives were accused of witchcraft and brutally murdered in Europe over a span of 300 years. That's a *lot* of extremely gruesome murders! I've had this same scenario come up for practitioner clients five or six times now.

Being burned at the stake seems to leave a very strong impression. When the reason for being burned at the stake is being recognized as a healer in one's community...well, you can imagine how this might create some reluctance to hang out one's shingle. Marketing one's practice may actually feel life-threatening.

I had Jean freeze everyone else in that terrible scene, right before the flames caught. Freeing her from the stake, we tapped on Jean's past-life self, discharging her terror, shock, anger, and feelings of betrayal.

In changing the picture, Jean's past-life self received help and was able to escape to safety in a neighboring country, where her healing talents were celebrated and highly prized. You can imagine the vast relief for both Jean and her past-life self. With the terrible threat gone, both women were able to pursue their healing practices.

Most of the past life selves I've encountered were victims of something extremely horrible. But on rare occasions, *they* were the perpetrator. One was a soldier participating in the massacre of a Native American tribe. Several were marauders, caught up in bloodlust while looting, raping and pillaging villages.

It takes real courage to confront a past-life self who is involved in a killing rampage of innocent women and children. One such brave client was "Jane," a small, soft-spoken woman in her late sixties. I was a bit nervous about this session. To be honest, I couldn't imagine how my somewhat frail client would take on this terrifying giant of a man. I imagined him lopping off her head or stomping her flat! It turned out I needn't have worried.

Jane stepped into the picture, and that warrior just stopped dead in his tracks. He actually fell to his knees before her and listened to her with grave attention. He allowed her to tap on him as she explained that he would have to pay for *all* of the terrible things he'd been doing (and yes, we used the simplest, most punitive idea of karma).

Although we couldn't elicit any empathy from him whatsoever, he did agree to change his ways – even though he expected to be attacked by his fellow marauders. He was somehow able to understand the karmic implications of his deeds and the thought of having to live through all of the pain and horror he'd been inflicting on others really sobered him up.

I have to admit I was amazed by this outcome until it occurred to me that this savage hulking warrior might be regarding my client as some sort of powerful supernatural or angelic figure. He was absolutely transfixed.

Afterward I mentioned this idea to my client, and she literally got goosebumps. She told me that was *exactly* how he'd been looking at her, though she hadn't realized it at the time. This explained why he'd been so willing to change the course of his life at her bidding.

Perhaps we really *are* playing the role of guardian angel when intervening in these past-lives. From our historical point of view, these past-life selves died a long time ago, so maybe that makes it more do-able. But what about loved ones who've died in our own, current timeline? Can we help them somehow? Stay tuned - our next two chapters explore working across the membrane of life and death.

CHAPTER 26

I See Dead People

Have you ever played peek-a-boo with a baby? It's adorable! You just hide your face behind a blanket and then pop out to say 'peek-a-boo'. For the baby, you pretty much cease to exist when they can't see you. When you suddenly reappear, the look of delighted astonishment on their face is priceless.

When it comes to death, most of us are like that little baby. Once we can't see our loved one anymore, for us, they've ceased to exist. But this is *much* less amusing than playing peek-a-boo. We tend to experience death as the painful, irrevocable loss of our loved one. And sure, they live on in our memories – a comforting thought, perhaps. But here's a better one:

People don't *really* die after all. Stay with me here...

Obviously, our *bodies* die. Accidents happen, we get sick, or they simply wear out. But the body is just something we wear for a little while. When we slip out of our body for the last time, our consciousness is intact.

What I'm getting at here is that our loved ones are still available to us. They may or may not be 'hanging around' all the time, but they can come in an instant if we ask them to show up.

This isn't just something I 'believe' is true. I'm not talking about religious faith or spiritual ideology. I've actually experienced this myself, and I've helped hundreds of clients reconnect directly with their 'dearly departed'. Not because I'm some kind of psychic or medium. This experience is available to anyone, especially while working in the Matrix.

Most of my work with clients involves trauma of one kind or another. Occasionally the trauma involves death – witnessing one, coming across a loved one who had died, or just getting the news over the phone. Very often this event triggers the Freeze Response, and so there's an ECHO or younger self.

Once we've done some tapping with this younger self to discharge their shock and distress, I'll have my client ask them if they'd like us to invite in the spirit of whoever just died. The answer is almost always an enthusiastic 'Yes!' Even if my client is a devout atheist, they're usually willing to at least humor me or to go along for the sake of their younger self.

In the Matrix, all that's required is to simply ask the spirit to show up. There are no real steps involved. Just a simple invitation and there they are.

I always ask my client whether the spirit seems to be radiating love, serenity, peace, joy, forgiveness or something like that. They always are, even if they were quite unhappy during their lifetime.

Spirits seem to be unencumbered by the difficult parts of their old personality. They keep their sense of humor if they had one, but they're free from the petty fears, anger, insecurities, jealousies, grievances, and doubts that may have plagued them while on Earth. Rather, they tend to have a peaceful 'mission accomplished' feeling, along with real compassion for those of us still going through it.

Meeting with our loved one's spirit is an opportunity to clear the air, to offer apologies, express anger, air grievances or ask for explanations. Often the younger self wants to know why their loved one had to die or die the way they did, and the spirit is able to explain. This can be incredibly healing when the death was a suicide. The spirit may offer an apology for how things worked out, but if my client or their younger self tries to apologize, the message is *always* that there's nothing to forgive.

Famous Last Words

I've done this now with at least a hundred clients. One of the first was Lisa, a woman in her early 60s. She actually came to me with crippling guilt because she'd put her ailing mom into a nursing home. They'd never really gotten along, lived on opposite coasts and her mom needed 24-hour medical care, but still, the guilt was overwhelming.

During the session a memory surfaced. For most of her life, Lisa had been burdened with the terrible memory of finding her dad sprawled out across his bed with a rictus of pain on his face. He'd died young, of a massive heart attack.

Lisa was 19 at the time and something of a rebellious punk rocker. Her last words to her father were "I hate you!" That was the proverbial icing on the cake. She'd unfairly blamed herself for breaking his heart and causing his death. Thank goodness she hadn't told him, "I wish you were dead!"

It took a fair bit of tapping on the 19-year-old, but we were able to discharge most of her shock, guilt, and distress. When we asked Dad's spirit to appear he showed up sitting on the bed next to the dead body. I guess he was something of a character because he thought that was hilarious.

He laughed away the 19-year-old's guilt over the "I hate you" remark, though he was very sorry my adult client had been so burdened by it all those years. He affirmed his love for her and apologized for the shocking manner of his death.

They were having a good old time when Mom walked into the room and saw the body of her dead husband – *but not his spirit*. Mom and Dad had had a bitter, contentious marriage. They'd long had their own bedrooms. In fact, that's how my client had discovered her dad. When he hadn't gotten up for work, Mom told her to go into his room to check on him.

Now Mom was in shock and overwhelmed with intense conflicting emotions. Naturally, I had Lisa tap on her mom, and as the distress began melting away, she let out a yelp! She could suddenly see her husband's spirit sitting on the edge of the bed, smiling at her!

They had their own reconciliation. Given their history, it was even more profound and beautiful than the 19- year-old's. I can't express how moving this was. A lifetime of anger, bitterness, guilt, and resentment just melted away in tears of forgiveness.

A few days later I got a message from Lisa that I'll never forget. She'd just received a phone call from her mom back east – a total shock because Mom had been bedridden, heavily medicated, on 24 hours a day oxygen and barely able to speak. She was expected to die at any time.

Mom's voice was strong. She was off the oxygen and walking now on her own. Her appetite had returned. She told her daughter she felt "a great weight had been lifted off her chest."

Lisa asked when this had come about, and Mom answered, "Three days ago in the evening." The time of our session! Her mom lived another six months and died peacefully in her sleep. I have no doubt at all that Lisa's dad was there to greet her on the other side.

Atheists Welcome

I've done this work now with clients of all religions and even hard-core atheists. Once the spirit shows up, there's never been the slightest doubt that it really *is* their loved one. I vividly remember one client, a 'recovering Catholic' who was extremely resistant to the whole idea – there *was* no after-life. That was all just a dirty lie.

She was definitely *not* interested, and I really had to lean on my rapport with her, but she'd been suffering from terrible grief over her sister's death, and I was determined. She was pretty grumpy about humoring me, but a few seconds into the scene her eyes flew open. She looked at me in shock and said, "That really IS my sister! I could *not* be making this up!"

Bringing the spirits in is some of the most beautiful, healing and moving work I get to do. And it's so easy! It's the ace up my sleeve when dealing with death trauma. I used to believe in 'life after death,' but now I know it's real – and that's very reassuring!

Grief as a Barrier

There's a book I recommend, *Journey of Souls,* by hypnotherapist Michael Newton. He'd regress clients back *in-between lifetimes* and then interview them, and the book is mostly transcripts from these sessions, which paint quite a consistent and illuminating picture. Really fascinating stuff.

In some of the session transcripts, spirits would describe trying to comfort and reassure their grieving loved ones but found their grief to be a nearly impenetrable barrier. Their messages of, "Hey, I'm okay, I'm still here!" were not received. This really caught my attention.

We think of grief as a natural emotion, something we're supposed to feel, and I'm sure that's true. But there's a common mistaken belief that if we let go of the pain around our loved one's death, we'll lose our connection with them – they'll fade away from our memory. Or that letting go of our grief would be dishonoring their memory.

On the surface, this may seem to make sense, but it's actually not true at all. Imagine you had a beloved dog for 14 years and when he got too old and sick, you had to have him put down at the vet. Now whenever you think of your dog, what comes up is that terrible trip to the vet, and all those terrible feelings of sadness and grief.

This means you aren't remembering all those times playing frisbee on the beach, snuggling in front of the fireplace, how cute he was as a little puppy or all the endless happy walks. All the good stuff is hidden behind a wall of suffering. Holding on tightly to grief does keep us connected – but connected to the *death* more than their life.

Pure Grief

When clients just can't let go of their grief, it's often because their sadness is contaminated by other feelings – usually some kind of guilt and/or resentment. These other feelings gum up the works, so to speak, preventing the natural expression of grief from running its course.

Cultural prohibitions against 'speaking ill of the dead' can inhibit us from processing anger, frustration, and resentment. We're not supposed to feel those things, let alone express them. So they're *not* expressed and get driven underground where they tend to fester.

I've also noticed a cruel irony around guilt – the people who least deserve it seem most inclined to experience it.

One client had spent six months caring for her dying mother. She'd been at her mom's bedside *constantly* for weeks but happened to be looking down at her phone when mom breathed her last. Her guilt was off the charts.

Another young client was pissed off at her dad in his last days. He hadn't put his affairs in order even though he'd known he was on his way out. She was his medical guardian but couldn't find any of the passwords for his accounts. Everything got dumped in her lap, but she felt she had no permission to feel angry.

She also felt guilty because once her father died, she'd finally be free to move away. His health had been failing for years, and she'd stuck around after college to help him out, putting her own life on hold. Part of her was impatient for him to just get on with it and die already. Totally understandable. But despite willingly sacrificing years for him, her guilt was crushing and only got worse after his death.

The good news is that these sorts of contaminating emotions can usually be tapped away very quickly. And then the grief can just run its course. The sadness can take on a kind of sweetness as it's balanced out with happier memories. And reconnecting with our loved one's spirit puts our loss into a whole new perspective. In the next chapter, I share some of my favorite spirit stories with you.

CHAPTER 27

Meetings with Remarkable Spirits

Some of my most fascinating sessions with clients involved bringing in the spirits of loved ones who'd died. Here are three I'd like to share with you.

A Rookie Win

It was the first day of one of my early Matrix training workshops. The students were in pairs doing their very first practice session, and Dahlia was the client in one of the dyads. She wanted to work on the trauma of her father's death some 20 years earlier.

Now in her mid-70s, Dahlia was still grieving her father on a daily basis. She described him as a truly exceptional man – kind, intelligent and loving. I got the sense that growing up he was the most loving, supportive person in her life – perhaps the *only* loving, supportive one. At any rate, she'd never gotten over his death.

Well, of course, I got very excited hearing this. They'd already tapped on Dahlia's younger self in the picture, so I whispered to her practice partner, "Just bring in her dad's spirit!" We hadn't covered that idea yet, so my student looked up at me with an expression of confusion and something like panic. With a bit of encouragement though, she gave it a try.

Without any fuss at all, Dad's spirit appeared for Dahlia's younger self. Within a few minutes, 20 years of daily grief was over. Her practitioner and I could see it melting away from Dahlia's face. Her father really *was* there with her! Dahlia's face began radiating joy.

She and her dad were able to say goodbye in a wonderful way, with the assurance that her father would be waiting for Dahlia upon her own death. This brought an incredible look of peace to her face. The whole thing took less than 20 minutes! Her practitioner was stunned.

The only downside was that Dahlia was toast for the rest of the day. Really for the rest of the workshop. But I think she got what she really came for.

A Ghost Story

Lizzy was 15 at the time of her father's death, and she was wailing. The scene was a hospital room, and the whole family was there – the doctors had just 'pulled the plug' on dad's life support machine. He'd been in a coma for quite a while and brain-dead for many days.

We tapped on the 15-year-old ECHO as usual, but when we invited Dad's spirit to show up something was wrong! I always ask my client is the spirit is radiating love and peace, and this time the answer was no! Lizzy said he looked confused and distressed. This had never happened before in any of my sessions. I was really taken aback – this was clearly *not* Dad's spirit. It took me a few moments to realize – this was his *ghost*!

According to *Journey of Souls*, after we die we return 'home' to debrief, review our lifetime, and get some R&R. We begin to remember who we really are while integrating our most recent personality and the lessons from our time on Earth. This is what's supposed to happen anyway.

Sometimes a person will die and not actually realize it. For various reasons, they simply don't get that they're dead. So, they tend to hang around *sans* body but stuck in their old limited personality. This is what had happened to Lizzy's dad.

He'd come to the hospital for routine surgery. It should have been no big deal, but there were complications, and he ended up on full life-support, eventually lapsing into a coma. He'd been 'brain-dead' for days before they finally pulled the plug. Even the doctors didn't know when he'd actually died.

At any rate, Dad's ghost had been stuck there, confused and unhappy. Luckily we were able to do some tapping with him and slowly help him understand that he'd died. He was rather reluctant to accept this and move on because so many people had depended on him. He'd been 'the rock' for his big family and a community organizer who'd helped hundreds of people.

We helped him understand that he was supposed to go off to 'central processing' to review his life and all that. *Then* he could come back and help his loved ones, but as it was now, he was actually doing more harm than good.

It became clear that he really needed someone to come and escort him back, someone he would trust. My client suggested his beloved aunt and uncle who'd died years earlier. So, we invited them in, and Dad finally did go off with them.

After we'd reimprinted Dad's beautiful departure, my client told me that her mom had been complaining for years about him being a poltergeist! Apparently, she'd find her undergarments thrown around the bedroom and pictures tipped over. She had no doubt it was him. Hopefully, our session put an end to whatever mischief he was causing.

Abandonment Resolved

Hannah was born right at the end of World War II. Her mother came from a poor farming family in Britain, and her father was a soldier from Eastern Europe, stationed near her village while the US, Britain, and Russia were hashing out the fate of his country.

Hannah's folks met at a dance and mom got pregnant that same night. Hannah's grandmother must have been a powerful woman. To save her daughter and the honor of the family, she was able to force a marriage to happen. Unfortunately, things didn't work out.

Hannah's father disappeared shortly after her birth. The family sent a delegation to his army unit but were told he was AWOL and considered a deserter. Soon afterward his unit was shipped back home. No one could say what happened to Hannah's father. They never saw him again.

This caused enormous hardship for my client's family. Dad's status as a deserter meant Hannah's mother would get no pension from the military. Worse still, she was unable to remarry, since there was no way to prove her husband's death.

Hannah's family became very poor, even by local standards, and in their tiny village, she was known as 'the bastard' growing up. Now in her 70s, she'd struggled with self-esteem and prosperity issues all her life.

We actually began our work by reimprinting Hannah's birth. In the new picture, her father was there, holding her. She'd never known her father in real life or even seen a photo of him, but that didn't matter, he really seemed to be there. They were able to bond, and it was very healing for her.

But after all of that, we still had half of our session time left. I suggested Hannah go back into the new picture we'd just created and ask her father what the hell happened to him. She did and began narrating what she was being shown.

Her father's spirit took her to stand beside him on the banks of a wild little river. He was pointing down into the water, and Hannah saw his body was somehow pinned under the surface by the strong current. He had drowned!

All in a moment I witnessed Hannah's face transform. Her father *hadn't* deserted them and runoff. Layer after layer of shame, abandonment, hurt and resentment melted away, softening her features, lightening her countenance. It was astonishing to watch.

We might have ended right there, so profound was the change. But her father's spirit had more to show her. Looking up from the sight of his body underwater, she saw he was pointing up at an old stone bridge spanning the little river.

Suddenly they were standing on the bridge, looking down on the body and she understood in a flash that he had jumped to his death. He'd actually killed himself! I worried that Hannah's feelings of abandonment would return, but instead, she was filled with great compassion. She simply asked him, "Why?"

His answer brought tears to both our eyes. He was able to show Hannah that he'd already had a family – a beloved wife and two children, who were murdered by the Nazis. He'd fought then in the war and had seen many terrible things. Like so many soldiers he'd been in a state of shock since the end of the war.

Being forced to marry again and going through Hannah's birth had re-triggered the unendurable pain and grief of losing his first wife and children. It became too much for him, and he chose to end his life. He hadn't realized the damage he'd be doing her and her mother and was profoundly sorry.

When she understood this, Hannah forgave him completely. Even this tragic knowledge of her father's life was incredibly healing for her. It *wasn't* her fault after all. She'd lived her whole life believing she'd been abandoned for being unlovable.

But we still had a happy ending to engineer! We couldn't have her dad *not* kill himself – that's against the rules. But we were able to change a few key elements. This time, instead of just slinking away from base, he let his commanding officer know that he was going out for a hike. In fact, he even showed him on a map of where he was headed.

When he didn't return, they sent out a search party and found his body. Since there was no evidence that he'd actually done himself in, the death was recorded as accidental. This meant that mom *did* receive a pension, which made their family one of the most prosperous in their tiny village.

And, of course, there was no talk of Hannah being a bastard. Especially after mom remarried and Hannah got to grow up with a father.

Essentially, we opened up a wildly different timeline for Hannah's little baby self. After all, Hannah had already suffered through 70+ years of shame, poverty, and abandonment; there was no need for her younger self to go through all that again! This is retrocausation writ large.

I like to think that we also did her father a great service, releasing him perhaps from a great deal of karma. I don't know for certain this is true, but it often feels that way to me when we're playing the role of angels like this.

A Gentle Nudge

Can you see how it didn't really take much of a change for things to work out vastly better for Hannah's younger self and family? Sometimes just a little shift can work wonders in the Matrix. Often just a bit of tapping, a little information, or just some basic encouragement is enough. People make better choices, lives change course, catastrophe is averted. Often these changes are the result of greater clarity and freedom to act on it. Shall we apply this now to your life? We've seen how EFT can dramatically enhance our freedom. In the next chapter let's focus on clarity of purpose - how would you really like your life to change?

CHAPTER 28

What Would You Like?

Imagine pushing a shopping cart through the supermarket, pointing at things on the shelves and saying, "I don't want that! I don't want that either. Oh man, I *really* don't want that one! Ugh. And look at that one, that's disgusting." Chances are you'd end up leaving the store with an empty cart.

People usually hire me because something is wrong. Maybe it's their relationship, or their career or weight or anxiety – *something* isn't going well. And honestly, they just want the pain to stop, the nightmare to be over, the self-sabotage to end. I'm the same way myself.

At some point though, we need to stop walking backwards into the future, turn around and actually choose a direction for ourselves.

When I first start working with a client, I like to ask, "If our work together is incredibly successful, what will change for you?"

Let me ask *you* the same question: If somehow this is the best possible book you could be reading right now, and it absolutely transforms your life, how will you know? What will change for you? Please take just a moment and notice what answers might come up for you.

Is it Okay to Want Things?

The Buddha is often misquoted as saying, "Desire is the root of all suffering." It's actually *attachment* to desire that is the problem. The more attached we are to an outcome, the stronger our disappointment, the more it hurts when we don't have it.

Attachment comes from a case of mistaken identity – we're convinced that we won't be okay unless we get what we're after. In other words, our experience of ourselves, our identity, is that we're incomplete. We're certain we *need* that possession, job, acclaim, lover, money, promotion or whatever it is, just to be okay. We *have* to get it, or else! And of course, none of this is true.

It sure can seem true though, and the suffering can be intense. This mistaken belief that *desire* causes suffering can really get in the way of setting goals. We don't want to get our hopes up. We won't let ourselves think big – to shoot for the moon. Aversion to disappointment and frustration can actually stifle our awareness of even knowing what we truly desire. Perhaps that's why so many people focus more on what they *don't* want.

Learning to let go of attachment can be really tough, but it's crucial if we want to allow ourselves strong desires and meaningful goals. Why? Because human beings are powerful reality generators. If *you* don't set your own intentions, there are plenty of other folks eager to tap your power by supplying their own agenda for you. We'll take a deeper look at how that works in the next chapter.

Why do I say you're a powerful reality generator? As a conscious, self-aware being your observations collapse probability waves all the time. Remember that double slit experiment, where they were trying to figure out whether electrons were like waves or particles? The outcome was subject to the experimenter's observation.

Schrodinger's cat is both alive *and* dead until we open the box to see. And, what you see depends very much on your intentions and expectations. Your expectations are based on the perceptual filters of your beliefs – whatever you've decided about yourself and about life. All of that stuff is getting projected onto the future by your subconscious mind.

Your intentions, on the other hand, relate to what you desire, which ideally is a *conscious* decision. Whenever you neglect to set conscious, deliberate intentions and goals based on your own true desires, you're basically letting your subconscious run the entire operation. In other words, you're on full autopilot.

Make no mistake, even when you *do* grab the wheel and chart your own course, your subconscious is still pretty much running the show! It's vastly more powerful than your dear little conscious mind. Honestly, the whole setting intentions thing is something of a negotiation. That's why it's so important to clear up whatever bad programming you've acquired through all those trauma capsules. You definitely want the subconscious on your side!

Without setting deliberate goals, the only real agenda will be reenactment. Imagine if when the Genie asked, "Master, what is your desire?" Aladdin had answered:

"I'd like to see more evidence that I'm unlovable."
"Please arrange a wonderful lover who'll reject me once she really gets to know me."
"After a lot of hard and frustrating work, I'd like to almost succeed but ultimately fail."

There go his three wishes. Not a very entertaining story, is it? Your subconscious mind is an amazing casting director – it can call in any number of new actors to play the same old roles, but let's keep it away from the screenwriting!

Sometimes what you *think* you want doesn't really make a lot of sense. It's important to delve into the 'why' behind your desire. The exercise below is a good way to get clear on what you're really after.

What Would *You* Like? An Exercise

Here's a simple exercise borrowed from NLP (Neuro-Linguistic Programming). It's great to do it with a friend, but otherwise, just grab a pencil and paper. Take a few moments to answer each question.

1. What would you like?

You don't need to overthink this. Just choose a goal, achievement or set of circumstances that's been on your mind. And write it down. Once you're clear on that, here's the next question:

2. What will having that do for you?

Really imagine having that thing or situation, and tune into what having that *does* for you. See if you can come up with a pretty clear answer. Again, take a moment and write it down.

3. Okay, so what will having *that* (whatever you just answered) do for you? Your answer may take you down to a more basic, fundamental level of what you really want.

4. And again, once you have a clear answer to that second round, ask again – what will having *that* do for you? (It's a lot easier to do this with someone else asking you the questions. But you get the idea).

Keep asking and answering, and eventually you're likely to get to a fundamental stopping place. Whatever it is will probably bring you some flavor of happy.

The next question is an interesting one:

5. And having *that*, what might go horribly wrong? Or you might ask a gentler question, "Is there a drawback or downside to having that?"

This is a way of exploring possible conflicts with having what you want – some hidden cost you might have to pay or something of value you might lose. If there *are* problems with having what you want, conflicts that might cancel out some or all of the benefits, it's incredibly useful to know what they are. This information is fertile ground for EFT tapping!

Here are some examples of how this process works.

Weight Loss

What would you like?
I'd like to lose weight!
And what will having that do for you?
I'll feel a lot more comfortable in my own body.
Great, and what will having that do for you?
I'll be more confident in the way I move in the world. I'll be more assertive.
Okay, and what will having that do for you?
I won't be so invisible – maybe I'll finally get promoted at work.

And what will having that do for you?
I'll feel good about myself. Successful.
And having that, what might go horribly wrong?
Hmmm. I guess if I stood out more people would expect more of me. There might be a lot more pressure, and I'm not sure how comfortable that would be. I might get really stressed out.

This is where it can be helpful to switch gears and go looking for a time when pressure brought about stress – and then tap on that memory.

Sales Success

What would you like?
I'd like to be more successful in my sales job.
And what would having that do for you?
Well, I'd make a lot more money!
And what would having that do for you?
I'd finally be able to buy my own home and stop renting. I hate paying someone else's mortgage off!
So, what will buying your own home do for you?
I'll be able to fix it up the way I want, plant a real garden, put on solar panels. I'll have something I can leave to my kids.
Great! And what will having that do for you?
I'll just be happy and content, I guess?
Okay, having your own house and fixing it up and all, what might go horribly wrong? (Tears come to his eyes at this point.)
"Well, me and the missus aren't getting along so well. We've actually talked about splitting up. I can't see us buying a place together at this point. I think we'd have to finally get divorced."

In the example above, do you think this fellow might be holding himself back from success in his sales job because he doesn't want to face divorce? And the woman who wants to lose weight, do you suppose she might be overeating because of anxiety that she won't be able to handle increased expectations?

Throwing Out a Line

I love the rather old-fashioned idea of having a 'calling' - the beautiful song of our heart's desire or the voice of our highest and best self- reminding us of our higher purpose. Once you've connected with that calling, even just a little, I have a lovely exercise for you in the next chapter to connect with one of your own Future Selves who has answered that '*calling*'.

CHAPTER 29

Meeting Your Future Self

A therapist, a life coach, and an EFT practitioner walk into a bar. The bartender looks up and says, "What is this, a joke?"

Do you know the difference between coaching and therapy? In general terms, coaching is all about identifying your goals and developing strategies for achieving them. In that sense, it's rather future-oriented. A coach also provides support, motivation and on some level holds you accountable for following through with your plan.

Therapy is more about making peace with your past so that it no longer defines your life or holds you back. Therapy can help address the root causes of procrastination, self-sabotage and the limiting beliefs that keep you playing small. A therapist can help a client set goals from a more empowered, authentic and grounded place.

I'm not a licensed therapist, but my own work is really more therapy oriented in that it's all about liberation from limiting beliefs, stuck emotions, and even physical problems that are rooted in the past. The deepest work I do involves my helping my clients' younger selves who are trapped, endlessly reliving some horrible moment.

But if we can work with younger selves from our past, what about connecting with *future* selves who are actually doing great? Future selves who have achieved some amazing goal? Who are living the dream, so to speak?

Not only *can* we connect with them, it turns out they can actually *help* us! In a sense, they are our ultimate life coach.

A Vision of Success

Think about some goal that you have – some image of real success. Some people might envision sitting across the table from their perfect mate. Or standing up on stage giving a TED talk. Or effortlessly running along the beach in radiant health. Or doing a book signing tour with a line out the door – their novel is on the New York Times bestseller list.

If you have a number of goals, that's great. But just for now, choose your favorite – the one that has the most juice, the one you most long for, your heart's desire. And closing your eyes, see if you can picture your Future Self enjoying that wonderful success. If you're not a visual person, that's okay. Just imagine the scene in whatever way works best for you.

If you *can't* really picture or imagine it, because it just seems impossible or you don't deserve it, or something like that – that means you've got some EFT tapping to do first. Make a list of all the reasons you can't have what you want and tap for each item. Give yourself some time for this, and come back to this Future Self business when things seem more free and open.

If you *can* picture your Future Self, enjoying that success you long for, here's a lovely exercise you might like to try. It's best to go through this with your eyes closed, so perhaps have someone read the instructions for you, or simply record yourself reading them out loud.

Close Encounters

Close your eyes and picture your future self as clearly as you can. If there are other people around, let's just freeze them in time. Now picture stepping into that scene as you are right now. Go to your Future Self and take her hand. Let her know that you are from her past and would like her help in getting to where she is now.

Once you have a good connection with her, ask if there's any advice, wisdom or information she can share with you. Listen carefully to hear what she says. Don't worry that maybe you're just making it all up. It doesn't really matter.

If you've already learned EFT, ask your Future Self to tap on you, to help remove any blocks you might have to being where she is now. As you imagine this, everywhere she taps on you, tap on yourself on that same point, allowing the words to come from her. Repeat them aloud or silently to yourself, either way, is fine.

Once the tapping is complete, ask your Future Self if you may step into her body, merging with her, taking on board all of her knowledge, wisdom, health, and vitality. Really let yourself feel this, and then unfreeze the scene and see yourself there enjoying it.

Once this merging takes place, you will now be established in the future self's scene. Take it all in, every aspect of that picture – the light, the sounds, the good feelings. Allow that picture to fill your mind and body and heart. Breathe it in and smile. Imagine broadcasting it back out from your heart into the Field around you.

This is a simplified version of an exercise created by Karl Dawson, the founder of Matrix Reimprinting. If you've only just read through the instructions and haven't tried it yet, perhaps it sounds simplistic or even silly. I'm sure I thought that myself until I experienced actually going through it.

What is Real?

Is your Future Self actually real? Real in the sense that you're not just making her up in your imagination? Hard to say, but probably. At least it really seems that way for most of my clients. They feel like they've had an actual encounter with an independent consciousness. And that was my own experience, even though I was skeptical going into it.

So what's going on here? How does it work? I don't pretend to really understand the quantum physics aspects of this, but what makes sense to me is that in every moment many potential alternate realities are branching out ahead of us. This relates to the idea of

Superposition – everything that can happen is happening until we collapse the probability wavefront.

And we do that every time we make a decision or even just an observation. We're inadvertently choosing a particular branch of reality to follow and all the rest collapse. On a fundamental level, this is how we create our own reality, and we're doing it all the time!

Anytime we set a goal, our intention imposes a general direction to follow in this ongoing unfolding of potentialities. We've established a destination, even if our current map doesn't show us a clear path from here to there.

Merging with a Future Self is goal-setting on steroids. Or really, goal-setting *personified*. Instead of the abstract idea of what we want, we're connecting with the person we will be once we're experiencing the accomplishment of that goal. We're literally identifying with them.

Our new connection with the Future Self informs the multitude of decisions we must make moment by moment, even if they're trivial or seem insignificant. There's a cumulative effect, and when our choices begin to lead us off and away, I believe there's a sort of magnetic pull or gravity, drawing us back in the right direction.

It's not unlike setting a destination in your car's GPS. If you make a wrong turn, it will simply re-calibrate the route.

This ongoing re-calibration will mostly be subliminal. Honestly, that's how almost all of our decisions are made anyway. In other words, connecting with your Future Self seems to enlist the aid of your incredibly powerful subconscious mind.

True confession – I often read through the exercises in a book but rarely go back and actually do them. Take it from me, don't skip this one. And hey, if you can't connect with some grand Future Self who's totally winning, perhaps you can connect with one from a few days hence who's ready, willing and able to go for it! How sci-fi is that?

Working with Future Selves, Past Life Selves and spirits of the dead can be absolutely amazing and transformative, but none of them has a physical body - at least not in our current time and space. But chances are very good that *you* do, along with most of the folks you hang out with. And let's face it, bodies can be problematic. That's why we're going to shift gears and kick off the next section of Hacking Reality dealing with body-related issues.

Part III

HACKING INTO HEALTH, WEALTH & HAPPY
RELATIONSHIPS

*"You are a child of God. Your playing small does not serve
the world. There is nothing enlightened about shrinking
so that other people won't feel insecure around you. We
are all meant to shine, as children do. We were born to
make manifest the glory of God that is within us."*
---Marianne Williamson

CHAPTER 30

Your Body is Not a Machine

Imagine coming across a car that's crashed up against a big old tree. Steam is still escaping the radiator, so it must have just happened. The whole area is closed off with yellow crime scene tape, and investigators are going over the car, taking careful measurements and trying to determine what went wrong.

By now a small crowd has gathered – there's going to be a press conference! Everyone wants to know what happened. Soon enough the lead investigator steps up to a podium and announces their official findings:

"We've determined that the engine was receiving too much gasoline while the brakes had insufficient pressure. This caused the car to travel at excessive speed whereupon it went into a skid and hit the tree."

All around you, people are nodding their heads approvingly, murmuring things like, "Of course! That explains it!" and, "Well sure, any fool can see it was going too fast" and, "Too much gasoline – just makes sense" and, "Glad they figured *that* out."

This, of course, leaves you feeling rather confused. What about the *driver?!* Was he drunk? Was he texting? Did he swerve to avoid hitting a squirrel? Did a bee fly in the window and sting him? What happened to make the driver crash?

So you shout out your question to the lead investigator, "Hey, what about the driver?" But he just looks at you blankly. Or simply rolls his eyes. The driver? Your question is absurd.

If you think of your body as the crashed car, for most of Western medicine there *is* no driver. The driver, what you think of as you, what might be called your consciousness, doesn't really exist.

Even if we admit that *maybe* the driver exists, it doesn't matter. It's all about the car. Even in medicine. Even in *psychiatry*. Why? Well, we can measure the car. We're really good at that. We can measure the car with ever increasing accuracy as we break it down into ever smaller component parts.

But we can't measure the driver. Belief in drivers is therefore unscientific. Mere religious superstition.

But let's get back to our crashed car and the official diagnosis – the engine was receiving too much gasoline and the brakes had insufficient pressure. Luckily there's a solution: the car needs a gas thinner. This will reduce the octane so it will have much less power. And a simple mechanical intervention can tighten the brakes so that they are on all the time.

Throw in a radiator transplant and a bit of cosmetic body work and we'll get that car back on the road.

Unfortunately, there are side effects – the brakes keep overheating. But there's a chemical fix for that: a simple silicone spray applied periodically with a newly patented device implanted in the wheel well. Thank goodness it's covered by insurance!

Also the engine is knocking pretty badly now due to the low octane gas. But hey, there's an additive for that. The additive causes a smoking exhaust problem which gums up the catalytic converter, but there's a newly approved second additive to control that smoking exhaust. Alas, it's very expensive, but a generic version will be out in a year or two.

The car has now become vastly more expensive to operate – a real cash cow for the automotive industry. Unfortunately, the driver actually *was* drunk when he hit the tree. A few months later he'll do it again and plow into a fire hydrant.

This is a ludicrous story, but it's really not that far off. For many folks caught up in the medical system, the treatment is sometimes worse than the disease. And the actual cause, having to do with attitude, emotions, and lifestyle, is never addressed.

The 'body is a machine' metaphor has been around so long that it's accepted by many people as established fact. It's the crown jewel of the materialist world view.

In this model, our body 'machine' has parts that can wear out and need repair or replacement. If something goes wrong with your body it's not your fault, you're just unlucky. You simply got bad genes – luck of the draw. But no worries, there's a pharmaceutical fix for whatever ails you. Or if that doesn't work, surgery, medical devices, artificial knees, etc.

Leave it to the medical mechanics; they'll get your car back on the road.

If *you* have physical issues to deal with, hacking reality means ditching this ridiculous metaphor. Machines aren't alive. They can't repair themselves – they require outside service and new parts. Even machines which are incredibly sophisticated have no consciousness. Your body is NOT a machine. Your body is an organism.

And that is good news because honestly, you're the one who needs a tune-up. Once you start tapping away the old stuck emotions and limiting beliefs, your body will be right there working with you to heal whatever is wrong.

Healing miracles can be surprisingly easy. Your body already *is* a miracle – manifesting out of space in this very moment. Releasing whatever static is interfering with the expression of your already perfect morphic blueprint is sometimes rather simple. The hardest part can be getting the rational mind to go along for the ride. We just have to coax it into the back seat so *you* can finally drive.

In the next few chapters, we'll explore ways of hacking the reality of your physical health.

CHAPTER 31

Hacking the Reality of Physical Issues

Important disclaimer – I am not a doctor. I'm not any kind of licensed health care practitioner. Nothing I write about here or elsewhere in this book is intended as medical, psychiatric or psychological advice of any kind. Please consult your doctor for any medical problems and especially before discontinuing any medications.

When a client shows up with some kind of physical issue, I usually run them through a fairly simple EFT protocol. I can't say it works every time – EFT is an amazing tool, but it's *not* a panacea and sometimes other healing interventions may be necessary. If someone just broke their leg, EFT isn't going to re-set the bone!

Step One: Tap on the Symptoms

Sometimes, even when it doesn't seem possible, symptoms just disappear with a few rounds of tapping. Why not go for it? It helps to be as specific as possible – really leverage those adjectives:
Even though I have this dull throbbing ache on the left side of my head, I deeply love and completely accept myself."
"Even though it feels like a cold, heavy gray lump of lead pressing down on the left side of my head, I deeply love and completely accept myself.

Sometimes, if you can reach without straining too hard, it can help to gently press into a painful area with your fingertips while tapping with the other hand:

"Even though it hurts right here where I'm pressing, right here under my fingertips, I choose to love and accept myself, and I forgive myself for anything I might have done to bring this about."

It might take three or four rounds of tapping to register any change. If there is improvement, don't be afraid to 'push your luck' – try to get the intensity level down to zero. Be persistent.

Sometimes Step One is all you need. But, just in case this doesn't work...

Step Two: Tap on the feelings

How do you feel *emotionally* about having this physical issue? Tapping away your negative intensity helps to 'get yourself out of the way' of the healing. Imagine asking someone with a twisted ankle how they feel about it – their answer might surprise you:

"Oh! I'm so angry I could spit! I must have told my daughter a thousand times to put away that goddam skateboard!" Or,

"I'm so embarrassed! I fell down in front of all my friends. There wasn't even anything to trip on! They must think I'm a total klutz, and I ruined our plans for the day. I can hardly face them." Or,

"It's terrifying. Is this the beginning of the end for me? What if I never fully recover? I'm sure I'll never enjoy walking again the way I used to."

Stressful feelings like these can be quickly tapped away, allowing the body to get on with the job of healing. To be sure, you have every right to be angry, or scared, or embarrassed, or whatever. You also have every right to let it go. EFT offers the means to do so.

Tapping your way into a more peaceful state might actually resolve your physical issue, or you might need to go back to Step One. And, this time, tapping on the symptoms can really work.

But just in case it doesn't...

Step Three: Investigation

What was going on in your life just before the injury or onset of illness? Often there was some sort of shock to the system that set things in motion – a loss, or feeling attacked, a sudden setback. If there *is* something, even if there's no clear connection with the physical problem, notice what feelings come up just thinking about it.

The idea here is to tap on every aspect of that event or situation until you get to a totally neutral place. This might take quite a bit of tapping! That said, resolving your feelings about whatever happened may help in ways that go beyond just the physical issue. Once you do, try going back to Step One.

Step Four: Upside to the Downside?

For really stubborn issues, it might be time for an honest look at possible benefits the problem gives you or possible downsides to letting it go. These can really get in the way of healing.

For example, a nurse worked with me on her terrible back pain. She'd been out on disability and was well aware of how much she was enjoying the break. In fact, she said she was tired of being a nurse and didn't want to go back! It was tough because her integrity required a genuine problem with serious pain. She couldn't just *pretend* to have back pain.

Having chronic migraines might mean a 'pass' from ever having sex with your disgusting husband. Or not having to go to those dreaded family events. Or, having them just melt away with a little tapping might validate what your horrible stepdad used to tell you, that you were making a big deal out of nothing.

This isn't about judging yourself! The subconscious mind works in mysterious ways, and many problems are also solutions to deeper problems. If there *is* some benefit to having the problem, tapping on the fear of losing that benefit, or the bad feelings around whatever situation it's protecting you from, can work a kind of magic. Space opens up for a resolution that may have seemed impossible.

Step Five: Examine Possible Metaphors

Jill was raised to be a good Catholic girl. As a young teenager, she began to chafe at all the expectations and decided to try out being bad. She'd gotten a job with a local doctor and somehow realized she could pad her time sheet, essentially stealing money that way. Very bad behavior! Naturally, she got caught right away.

We were doing some tapping on the traumatic scene of being confronted by the doctor and nurse, who were threatening to call the police. It was a moment of great shame and fear for her younger self, and still very emotional for Jill decades later. As we tapped through the points I just happened to use the expression, "*caught red-handed.*"

Jill's eyes flew open, and she held out her hands to me, showing her palms. She practically yelled, "Is *that* why I've had this eczema on my hands all these years?!"

This was news to me. She'd never mentioned eczema before. And now, staring at her palms I had to ask, "What eczema?" I couldn't see anything unusual. When she looked at her own palms she was astonished, "It's gone!"

Apparently, Jill had had itchy red bumps on her palms for the past 20+ years. They were a source of great embarrassment to her. She was in the habit of hiding her palms, which is probably why I'd never noticed any problem. Now, simply tapping on the words "caught red-handed", the bumps were gone, and they didn't come back – at least for the next five years or so we were in touch.

We have so many 'figures of speech' that seem to relate to physical problems. If someone has a sharp pain in the middle of their upper back, what does that bring to mind? Ask them if they've been betrayed recently and they'll likely say "Yes!" They were 'stabbed in the back' by someone they'd trusted.

When someone says they have a pain in their neck I like to ask, "What's his name?" This often provokes a laugh because there really *is* someone. Lower back pain often translates to feeling unsupported – 'no one has my back'. Shoulder pain might come from feeling burdened – 'carrying the weight of the world.'

Unwillingness to honestly look at what's going on – 'turning a blind eye', can lead to vision problems. Refusing to hear something – bad news, criticism, the unvarnished truth. Might that affect our hearing?

I've had several clients with diabetes who had a serious issue with receiving love and affection – the 'sweetness' of life. Foot problems often relate to fears of taking the next step, or 'standing my own ground.' Even the sentiment, 'I just can't stand it' could show up in the feet or legs. Restless leg syndrome may be the somaticized conflict between wanting to move forward and holding one's self back.

What's the hell is going on here? How can this possibly be real? Remember, the subconscious mind runs every aspect of our physical body. And there's no rational, critical intelligence in the subconscious. None whatsoever. It tends to take our words quite literally. Especially cultural clichés. And most especially when they're emotionally charged.

Don't get me wrong, I'm not saying the associated physical problems aren't real. They're absolutely real, but when the *cause* comes down to a subconscious misunderstanding, sometimes a little tapping can work wonders.

So there you have it – your 5-step protocol for hacking into the reality of physical issues to tap them away. As mentioned, sometimes it still doesn't work. But when it does, the results can be totally mind-blowing.

And for that reason, I'm including a special bonus step for you...

Helping the Rational Mind Adjust

Poor old rational mind – it really doesn't like miracles. They're very unsettling because they don't make sense. The changes just aren't possible! That's not how things *work*.

If you do manage to pull off a miracle for yourself or someone else, that change is likely happening on the quantum level. But your rational mind is stuck in the old Newtonian model of reality. Sometimes it's actually important to help it adjust. We don't want the silly old thing to sabotage our lovely results. Happily, there's a fairly easy way to address this with some simple tapping:

Start with a set-up statement such as:

Tapping on the karate chop point:
"Even though this can't be real, it must be some kind of weird trick, I sure wish it was real – that would be fantastic!"

And then, tapping through the points:
"But that's impossible! That's not how the body works. That can't have happened. And yet, my pain actually is gone right now. And that's wonderful! But it's probably going to come right back. It can't be that easy. This change can't be permanent. But I sure wish it was. My pain can't just go away – I saw the X-rays. The problem is real. It's physical. The doctors said so. There's no way this improvement can last, the pain is going to come roaring back as soon as I walk out that door. But it's gone right now. It really is. It doesn't make sense, but it went away. I sure wish it would stay away."

Addressing the doubts and concerns of the rational mind with tapping seems to take the edge off and helps the amazing change stick. If the change is truly 'unbelievable,' like a rotator cuff problem vanishing, or bone on bone knee pain going away, I'll often tap in a reminder of the energetic nature of their body, how it's appearing out of space in every moment based on a perfect blueprint.

I'll explain more about this perfect blueprint in the next chapter. But, meanwhile, here's an example of this sort of tapping so you can try it out yourself:

Blueprint Tapping Script

Tapping on the karate chop point:
Even though my pain is totally gone and that doesn't make any sense, I wish it would stay away, I feel so much better

And tapping on the points:
My pain is gone!
that's impossible
that doesn't even make sense
this tapping doesn't have anything to do with my injury
it can't be that easy
but I sure wish it was
the pain will probably come right back
this has to be some kind of weird trick
but I have to admit it's gone right now
even if it did come back, maybe I could tap it away again?
it just doesn't make any sense
that's not how the body works
no one can heal from an injury like mine that fast
it takes a long time
and it's *been* a long time- I've been so sick of that pain!
it can't be that easy
but the reality is, every cell in my body is made out of molecules
and every molecule is made out of atoms
and every atom in my body is made of subatomic particles
and all of those particles are made of energy
energy that's winking in and out of space
every part of my physical body is actually just energy
appearing out of space in every moment
and there's a blueprint for my body
that tells every particle of every atom how to manifest as me
and that blueprint is perfect
my injury never changed the blueprint
but my injury *did* create static in the field
and that static interfered with the printout that is my physical body
and now that static is gone
it's been tapped away
I can *feel* that it's been tapped away
and now my body can appear again in it's perfect form
and so it is...

CHAPTER 32

Healing in the Field

James was asleep in the back seat when the cars collided head-on. It was 2 a.m. on New Year's Day after a night of partying. He was just 21. Miraculously the other three people in the car escaped with barely a scratch. James was not so lucky.

The crash shattered his right femur, held together now with seven titanium pins. When we met, it had been a little over two years since the accident and James had been in severe pain ever since. He'd become addicted to Vicodin and then struggled to wean himself off again, but the pain was unbearable, making a normal life virtually impossible.

I was new to Matrix Reimprinting, and this was one of my first phone sessions. At first, it seemed fairly routine. I had James step into the scene and connect with his younger self, just as the crash was ended.

His younger self was in the smashed up car with part of his scalp ripped off and hanging down in front of his face! That was gory. I had James put it back in place and then simply wave his hand over his younger self to take away all of his physical pain.

Removing pain is a neat trick we can do in the Matrix. It allows us to focus more on the emotional intensity and whatever decisions were being made in the moment of Freeze. Which is exactly what we did with James' younger self – tapping away the terror of waking up to the chaos and violence of the crash.

James let his younger self know that his three friends were all okay, just a little banged up but none of them injured. That was a huge relief. Once he was out of shock, it was time to ask James' younger self how he'd like the scene to change. You might guess that he wanted the wreck to have never happened, but luckily he didn't.

Instead, he asked to not be injured. After all, his three friends walked away pretty much unscathed. Why shouldn't he?

To be honest, I didn't know what to say. It didn't seem right to me. I mean the guy has *titanium pins in his leg*. They're not going to just disappear. Changing the picture so drastically seemed wrong somehow like it would be breaking the rules. But for the life of me, I couldn't think of anything else to suggest.

So I just sat there, my mind racing, but absolutely *nothing* else was coming to me – no alternative suggestion. After what seemed like a very long time, I finally gave up and said, "Okay. Just pull him up out of the wreckage, dust him off, and he's fine."

In the new picture that we reimprinted, James and his friends were standing by the side of the road near the smashed up car, waiting for a taxi to come pick them up. They were laughing at how lucky they'd been. I was feeling *deeply* concerned with this outcome until James opened his eyes and said, "The pain is gone!"

For the first time in two years, James felt absolutely no pain in his leg. It was totally gone. And didn't come back, at least not in the next three weeks. I checked back in with James several times, but then he took off on a trip, and I didn't hear from him again.

Over the years I've had similar results with many clients, where chronic pain from an injury turned off like flipping a switch. It took me a while to figure out how that works, though in hindsight it seems rather obvious. It's all about the Freeze Response.

We've already looked at how the Freeze Response opens up a wormhole in our normal experience of space and time. The feelings of our younger self can come flooding right into our body now through this open channel. We feel their emotions as if they're our own, even though they may be wildly disproportionate to our current circumstances.

Well, it works the same way with *physical* feelings. When a physical injury coincides with the Freeze Response, the younger self's pain can come into our body as easily as their emotional feelings do.

This is why normally effective treatments don't always work for these chronic conditions. If I'm feeling the physical pain of my younger self, the massage *I'm* getting isn't helping him. The acupuncture, chiropractic adjustment or even the pain meds I'm taking now don't do anything at all for my younger self, and he's the source of my pain.

So I feel pain even if there's nothing wrong with me physically. Even if my body has long since healed from the original injury, *he's* still in pain. And that pain is still coming into *my* body. Once we discharge the Freeze Response for that younger self, the wormhole shuts down, and the pain is gone.

When I was first exploring this strange phenomenon, a question came up for me: Is it possible to be injured *without* going into the Freeze Response and creating a trauma capsule? In fact, without even noticing the injury? The answer is yes!

I've done a fair amount of construction work over the years and generally find it enjoyable and satisfying. Sometimes though at the end of the day, I'll be taking a shower and suddenly realize I've got a massive bruise or nasty cut on my leg! I'd spent the day happily working away, totally in the 'zone' and never even knew I'd injured myself.

I've noticed that those kinds of cuts and gashes, where there was no Freeze Response, never seem to leave a scar. My body just heals itself quickly and automatically, with no trace left behind.

The Tipping Point

Just to be clear, not *all* chronic pain conditions stem from a single traumatic injury. Lower back pain, for example, may arise from many events that left us feeling unsupported. This can build up over a long period of time. Our subconscious mind is absurdly literal and may somaticize our emotional conflicts.

These metaphoric conditions can sometimes be tapped away very quickly, but more commonly a number of related memories need to be surfaced and resolved. In other words, it might take longer, and instead of simply switching off, the problem might be more apt to slowly fade away, once a 'tipping point' has been crossed.

Remember there's a morphic field for your body, a blueprint or pattern that tells all of the subatomic particles how to coalesce into the atoms in your body, and how to put themselves together into your skin and bones and organs and such. However solid and stable it may seem, your body is also appearing out of Space in every moment, essentially made out of energy.

Unless you were born with some rare genetic problem, your blueprint's 'factory default settings' are for perfect health. If we look at the 'printout' of your actual physical body, however, it may be a little wonky. Or seriously messed up. Perhaps your eyesight has deteriorated. Or you have arthritis, or plantar fasciitis, or a tumor, or any number of problems. Why is this?

In the space between the blueprint and the printout we often find a sort of static. This static can disrupt or distort the signal your blueprint is sending. It doesn't *change* the blueprint, but rather interferes with the reception.

The static, of course, is made up of unexpressed emotional intensity and unhealthy belief structures held in place by the Freeze Response. Depending on the intensity, or even just sheer quantity of these trauma capsules all kinds of weird patterns get set up in our physical manifestations.

This static might show up overnight as the result of some spectacular trauma. Or from a slow build-up of relatively minor but recurring, self-reinforcing bad experiences. Once it reaches a certain level, it can wreak havoc in your body.

The good news is that our original blueprint never changes. The 'factory default settings', if you will, are essentially perfect and we can return to health simply by removing the static. When this can be done all at once, we're likely to see healing 'miracles' like spontaneous remissions. More often though, the 'static removal' is a process and healing is gradual until we finally reach that tipping point where the return to health becomes inevitable.

I've come to appreciate the reality of this because I've seen clients experience dramatic physical healing even though we weren't even addressing physical issues. Here are a few stories for you.

Inadvertent Healing

After 12 sessions dealing with intense childhood abuse and trauma, Lily told me that her allergies were all gone. I had no idea that she'd *had* any allergies and told her so. "Oh yes! I used to take Claritin every day!" Even though we'd never addressed her allergies directly, apparently their cause had been resolved. For the first time in her life, the world felt like a safe place.

Rachel wore thick 'coke bottle' eyeglasses. We'd cleared a lot of bad memories but had never tapped on her poor eyesight. One day she came to me straight from an eye exam with a new optometrist. He'd told her that her old prescription was much too strong. Since eyesight isn't supposed to get better, he must have thought her previous optometrist was totally incompetent!

Rachel knew otherwise. Her vision *had* improved. That's why she sought this new guy out. She felt that her old optometrist wouldn't be able to accept the change, and she didn't want to deal with his resistance. Rachel was certain the change had come from clearing so much of her childhood trauma.

Debra came to me wanting to resolve being molested as a young teen. Clearing that memory turned out to be a 'one session wonder.' I heard from her months later that she'd lost 40 pounds – and this had happened without even trying! Apparently, her appetite and metabolism had changed, without Debra even realizing it. Her body must have finally felt safe again to be slender.

Even if there's no obvious connection with a physical issue, resolving our worst memories seems to be a wonderful gift for our physical body. It removes all kinds of stress for sure, but along with that, developing a happier, more peaceful and empowered experience of life is really good medicine.

CHAPTER 33

Autoimmune Disorders

In researching this book I was surprised to learn how many diseases are actually considered autoimmune disorders, including Lupus, Rheumatoid Arthritis, Multiple Sclerosis, Hashimoto's and many others. Weirdly enough, Fibromyalgia and Chronic Fatigue Syndrome are not currently on the official list, though they certainly seem to fit the description.

Our immune system is tasked with the crucial job of identifying and neutralizing specific threats to our bodies. 'Autoimmune' means that this system has been misdirected and instead of dealing with dangerous bacteria or viruses, it's actually attacking some part of our own body, a bit of inflamed joint tissue for example. This then sets off a cascading chain reaction of symptoms, leading to a vicious circle of pain, weakness, and disability.

I've come to believe that the root cause here is almost always FEAR, in the form of a strong epigenetic danger signal being broadcast 24/7 from an ECHO, or host of ECHOs, who are experiencing some kind of terror. It's like an internal air raid siren going off:

DANGER!

DANGER!

DANGER!

Although the incident may have taken place many years ago, because of the Freeze Response it registers with the body as a current event. The danger signal may have been muted for years by the dissociation of the trauma capsule, but some shock in our current life causes it to breach. Or ongoing stress drains too much energy from our system, and there's not enough left to keep the capsule sealed up. Either way, the alarm signal begins to leak out.

Our immune system is primed to tune in and react to these signals. It can't understand that *the bad thing already happened*, that this is a signal from our past. For the immune system, the threat is immediate, and it *has* to respond!

Ask someone with fibromyalgia if they think the world is a safe place and they'll likely laugh out loud. What a stupid question! Of course not! How absurd. This reaction is a giveaway of decisions made by their younger selves who were faced with some terrifying experience:

People are dangerous.
The world is not a safe place
Something bad will happen
It's not safe to relax

The peculiar thing is, when I ask these clients how they *know* the world is a dangerous place, it's a bit of a mystery. It seems that nothing really bad ever happened to them. Certainly nothing traumatic. Their parents were loving and supportive. They had a wonderful, uneventful childhood. Aside from their debilitating condition, everything is just fine and always has been.

I've heard this so consistently I've pretty much come to expect it. My guess is their dissociation from traumatic events is so 'successful', they're running 100% of the emotional distress through their physical body.

No Big Deal

As much as I'd like to believe their *#nothingbadeverhappened* story, my clients hire me to help them. I've got a job to do, dammit. And sometimes that means badgering them to open up and spill the beans. With Angie, this badgering took about half of the session.

Angie told me she was recently put on disability due to fibromyalgia. She actually liked her work, but just couldn't manage with the pain and fatigue. She'd had symptoms for the past seven years, but they kept getting worse. Her doctor couldn't do anything more for her, so she wanted to give EFT a try. Not that she was hopeful I could help her. This was just another weird alternative thing to check off the list.

The obvious question here is, "What might have been going on in your life in that time before the fibro first kicked in?" Of course, the answer was "Nothing." After almost 45 minutes of coming back to that question, she finally told me, "Well, there was this one thing... but it's no big deal."

The 'No Big Deal' happened a few months before the fibromyalgia started. Angie was in her early 20s, still in college, and having a conversation with her boyfriend, who happened to be on the football team. She was on the cheerleading squad. He was huge, and she was petite.

They were over at his mom's house, just talking about this or that, when suddenly he flipped out and began screaming at her, and then hitting her. She found out later he'd been injecting testosterone and was probably on speed as well.

Angie fought back and even kicked him in the balls, but he was really big and strong to start with, and the drugs gave him manic strength on top of that. While slapping her and shaking her around like a ragdoll, he finally smashed her head against the brick fireplace and knocked her out.

Well sure, that sounds like 'no big deal' right? *But wait, there's more.*

When Angie came to, she was outside wrapped up in a blue tarp, and her boyfriend was pouring gasoline over her! Apparently, he had some drug-addled idea of burning the evidence. He was about to burn her alive! Fortunately, his mom drove up just at that moment, and Angie was able to escape.

While she'd been unconscious, he'd continued beating and kicking her. She was so badly injured she had to go to the emergency room, where it was discovered he'd also raped her. She soon found herself pregnant and opted for an abortion.

At the end of this harrowing tale, do you know what she told me?

"But I dealt with all that in therapy."

Angie really thought that was true! Because she could remember and re-tell the story with little or no emotional intensity, she genuinely thought it had been resolved. It hadn't. She'd actually 'dealt with all that' by having fibromyalgia.

I had Angie picture her younger self moments before getting knocked unconscious. We froze her scary boyfriend, and I asked Angie to step into that scene as her current self and take her younger self's hand. The instant they touched Angie's intensity level shot from zero to ten+. Her feelings of terror and helplessness were truly off the scale. This was a total shock for Angie, who really had thought it was 'dealt with'.

We actually did deal with it by tapping on Angie's younger self, discharging her terror and getting her out of the Freeze Response. As I recall the positive new picture felt very empowering and may have included a taser. It took us so long to get going, we didn't have enough time left to do the tarp and gasoline bit. But the new picture we managed felt pretty solid.

A One Session Wonder

When I checked back in with Angie a few months later, her symptoms had mostly all faded away, and after seven years of increasing pain and disability, she was getting ready to return to work. But how did Angie's symptoms get better from this one session?

To try and answer that question, allow me to recap how I think this works. But first I should mention that having one singular trauma made this a relatively easy case. It's not always so clear what happened, and sometimes there are a lot of traumas involved.

When Angie was being assaulted by her boyfriend and overwhelmed by helplessness, she flipped from Fight or Flight straight into the Freeze Response. A part of her, what we call the ECHO or younger self, split off to "hold the trauma."

Angie's younger self had been trapped there, endlessly reliving that experience for the past seven years. Her feelings of terror were extreme, but to make matters worse, she'd been attacked by the person she was most intimate with. Her younger self decided that Life Isn't Safe, You Can't Trust *Anyone* and The People You Love Will Turn on You and I Can't Protect Myself.

These beliefs kept Angie in a constant state of stress, making it that much harder for her body to relax and re-regulate.

Talk therapy had helped Angie make peace with the memories, in a sense. But really that just meant putting a tighter lid on the can of worms. The terror was always running just below the surface, sending out that very powerful epigenetic '*DANGER!*' signal.

Angie's immune system must have been frantic to protect her. It didn't know the signal was coming from past events, and so it kept looking for *something* to defend against. Since there wasn't any real-time intruder, it eventually found some part of her own body to attack. But the signal kept coming, and so her immune system redoubled its efforts, eventually causing so much inflammation and pain she could barely function.

Our one session together turned that signal *way* down. To turn it all the way off we probably needed to do 'part two' and maybe a memory or two from childhood. But the work we did do was enough for Angie's immune system to stand down so her body could recover. Despite our success, Angie never did want to follow up and resolve the second part of her 'no big deal' trauma. I guess getting back to work was good enough.

Let me be clear – I'm not saying that some terrifying trauma is the root cause for *every* autoimmune disorder. Other issues or problems might dysregulate the immune system. However, I have seen this same pattern consistently, so my first line of inquiry is to ask a client, "Is the World a safe place?" It might be worth asking yourself that same question.

Cancer

Cancer sucks. We all hate it. In fact, our current Western approach to cancer is intensely adversarial. Cancer is the enemy. One battles cancer. One puts up a brave fight. Our treatments are all about attacking and destroying cancer cells. We cut it, burn it and poison it. We've declared WAR on cancer, though victory seems ever elusive.

Our 'war' is being fought on a physical battlefield, with research focused on the biochemical aspects of the disease. We're seeking material solutions, and I sincerely hope that we find them. But are there *non-material* aspects of cancer we might be addressing?

Recent discoveries about the role of epigenetics in gene expression suggest that emotions, attitudes, and beliefs may play a part in developing cancer. Feelings cause physiological changes in the body. That isn't some far out woo-woo theory. It's a measurable fact. And it should be obvious by now that our attitudes and beliefs influence our feelings.

This is what I'd like to explore with you here. It's not an either/or situation – by all means, let's keep on investigating all manner of material interventions! But what about the other stuff?

The Cancer Profile

A few years ago, one of my clients made me aware of Dr. W. Douglas Brodie's cancer personality profile. She'd been diagnosed with terminal cancer and felt he was describing her life with uncanny accuracy.

As Dr. Brodie puts it: "In dealing with many thousands of cancer patients over the past 28 years, it has been my observation that there are certain personality traits present in the cancer-susceptible individual."

Those most prone to getting cancer, according to Dr. Brodie, are often caretakers who put the welfare of others first. Sometimes just one particular person. Dedicated to shouldering the burdens of others, making them happy or at least comfortable, caretakers are highly conscientious with a strong sense of duty. These are compassionate, caring people who don't seem to have a mean bone in their body.

But sometimes there's a dark side.

Underlying their dedication to service may be an element of fear. These are 'people pleasers' who often sacrifice their own well-being in the quest for approval. Growing up with one or more emotionally distant, needy and/or highly critical parent can cause this because trying to win their approval really isn't optional. It's a matter of survival.

Or so it seems to the young child. Fear of displeasing Mom and/or Dad creates a hypersensitivity to the needs of others. And this becomes one's default mode for living. Walking on eggshells. Living outside of one's own skin. Self-awareness of the caretaker's own personal needs may barely register.

"Don't be selfish!" would have been a terrifying and oft-heard scolding, taken to heart. The message is very clear: One must live *only* for others.

For children caught up in this dynamic, their own natural anger and resentments register as dangerous, threatening that all-important parental approval. These feelings can be repressed so successfully that adult caretakers may have no awareness or access to them. They don't *do* anger. This leaves them unable to set healthy boundaries and thus vulnerable to exploitation.

This is a big problem. Walled off feelings that can't be acknowledged or expressed don't just go away. They fester, becoming toxic. Almost like a tumor!

Experiencing one's inner landscape as toxic and unacceptable is a set-up for isolation and loneliness. No one must be allowed near! Serving others becomes the only legitimate way to connect. Cancer Profile caretakers are often adept at finding one-sided relationships, where they can serve without having to accept anything in return.

Imagine how stressful it must be to live this way. Especially when there's an element of perfectionism in the winning of approval. Even the mundane challenges of day to day life become draining and oppressive. And, ironically, caretakers are rarely willing to ask for help or accept it. They suffer in silence, feeling the weight of the world slowly crush all the joy out of their life, perhaps inadvertently losing their will to live.

Often an especially stressful event occurs in the months before the onset of symptoms – the proverbial last straw. It may be some significant loss that's totally beyond their control. Their entire strategy for managing life seems to utterly fail, and they have no way left to cope.

Sometimes the relationship with the person they are caring for becomes so oppressive and draining, and they feel so utterly trapped, that DEATH seems like the only escape. A lifelong terror of upsetting anyone means suicide is not an option, so on a deeply subconscious level, cancer becomes the ultimate solution.

Just to be clear – I'm not saying that merely being a caretaker means you'll get cancer. And many who do get cancer don't fit Dr. Brodie's profile. There may be lots of other factors. But isn't it worth looking into, when helping someone with cancer?

Be All You Can Be

Along these same lines, my dear colleague, Forrest Samnick, wrote the following as a Facebook post some years ago:

> A dear friend of mine died yesterday after being diagnosed with Stage IV lung cancer just two weeks ago. She was 50 years old. I have this profound sense, and quite a bit of empirical knowledge, that cancer is about producing more of self. When we deny ourselves from following our heart's desires by placing others' happiness and desires before our own, we start to lose

who we are. The body's response is to create more of who we are. The clients I have had with cancer who are able to hear this message from the body and take the steps to create a loving relationship with self almost always heal. My friend had a lot of dreams but was afraid to make the necessary changes in her life to make those dreams come true. Death of someone we love reminds us that life is fragile and the time to create the life we want is now. It is your life, please don't live it for someone else

Publish or Perish

Sandy was a gifted EFT practitioner and one of the first graduates of my Academy. When she walked into my office for an appointment, I was shocked. Her skin was chalky white and her eyes sunken and dry. She looked absolutely terrible. She'd just received a diagnosis of Stage 4 uterine cancer. They'd given her about two months to live.

Sandy was put on Hospice straight away, her only treatment palliative care for massive pain. She was on several heavy-duty painkillers, including methadone, but they weren't working very well. She came to me for help with the pain and the intense fear she was feeling. We got right to work.

Sandy always responded very quickly to tapping – by the time she walked out the door, 90 minutes later, her pain had dropped 80 percent along with her fear level. Amazingly, her face looked normal again, color had returned, and she was smiling and laughing. We'd also identified the possible cause of her cancer.

A month or two before cancer showed up, Sandy had abandoned her life's work – a memoir she'd been working on for 14 years. This was the third time she'd given up on her book, and the third time she'd developed cancer shortly after that. It may seem incredible, but Sandy had never made that connection before!

Shortly after receiving an MFA degree in literature, she made her first decision to abandon her memoir. Her graduate program left her demoralized and convinced she had no talent as a writer. She casually mentioned, "After I gave up the book it was like I had nothing left to live for." Her body seemed to agree, and a few months later she was dealing with breast cancer.

Having survived chemo and radiation, Sandy took up the book again and after a few more years had nearly finished it. She'd scored a "fancy pants agent" in New York City who loved the draft she'd sent and was in the process of landing her a big contract. It was amazing good fortune, but Sandy freaked out and walked away from the deal *and* the book. Six months later the breast cancer returned.

This third bout of uterine cancer was the most serious yet. After a long break, she'd been rewriting the book again, doing a major revision and decided once more to stop. She'd actually talked seriously about burning the manuscript! In our second session, we set about exploring Sandy's apparently life-threatening writer's block. It was quite a story. As they say, you can't make this stuff up.

Sandy had grown up in the Midwest. Her mother really should have been a writer. She'd won two national awards from the *Atlantic Monthly* while still in high school which led to a full scholarship at Oxford! An incredible opportunity for a small-town girl but she turned it down to marry Sandy's father. Together they had five kids.

Growing up, Sandy learned that writers were selfish, narcissistic people. Caring for others was what gave life meaning. And as the oldest girl of five, Sandy had plenty of opportunity for *that* sort of meaning.

Early on, Sandy became mother's little helper – cleaning house, doing the dishes and helping with sewing and cooking, while the boys were out playing baseball and having a good old time. Sandy's cute little sister somehow never quite joined the housework team. She took dance lessons instead.

Sandy's father was a poet. Except that he never actually published any poems. As far as Sandy knew, he'd never even written any! But no one was supposed to outshine dad. This was an unspoken rule in the family. *He* was the 'creative one', and all five kids learned not to shine very brightly. Mom saw to that.

This is what Sandy had been up against. She'd been assigned the role of caretaker early on and being a successful writer would be a deadly insult to both her parents. But there was even more to the story.

It turned out Sandy's memoir was pretty racy – full of her own sexual exploits in the 60s and 70s. Embarrassing to think of mom and the family reading all that! But there was another darker bit about being molested by one of her older brothers – too important to leave out, but certain to cause pain and drama. This was the reason Sandy had walked away from that publishing deal.

After a few more sessions Sandy let go of Hospice. She still had the tumor, but the pain was mostly gone, and she was off her pain meds. She was writing again and making good progress. Friends let her use their remote beach cabin on the Marin coast for a week-long writer's retreat.

I wish this story had a happier ending, but Sandy ended up dying of cancer anyway about six months later. For years she'd wanted to visit John of God in Brazil. Feeling so much better she decided to go for it and booked a month long stay, hoping for a spiritual healing.

She did have a powerful spiritual experience there, but by the time she came home all of her symptoms had returned in full force. She went back on Hospice and died a few months later. It was a sad turnaround, but Sandy's attitude toward death was incredibly positive and uplifting. To her friends she wrote:

> *It's time. This is my next step, and I want to take it. I'm not afraid of it. I know the moment of passing over will be a moment of great relief and ecstasy. I understand sorrow and grief will be a natural reaction, but please know that there's no need to feel any on my behalf. I am excited! Thank you ALL for being in my life! We will meet again...*

Before she died, Sandy told me a friend would be tackling her book, publishing it posthumously if it could be wrestled into good enough shape. I don't know if that's really going to happen but would dearly love to hold a copy in my hands.

Alternative Treatments

I would never offer anyone medical advice of any kind and nothing in this book is intended as such in any way. That said, many of my clients dealing with cancer are looking for alternatives to chemotherapy, radiation, and surgery. They often fear being railroaded into treatments that have significant side effects and surprisingly low success rates.

I've learned from my clients there are many promising alternatives, often inexpensive and readily available. A diligent Google search (try using the term 'promising') might reveal some very interesting suggestions, coming from both serious scientific studies and credible personal accounts.

To get the most powerful results from EFT tapping, my suggestion is to start with the fear and don't hold back! Go after every aspect of fear the cancer brings up, including fear of death. Make sure and tap on the shock of receiving your diagnosis. This is exactly what reduced Sandy's pain and fear so dramatically.

I'm not saying tapping will cure your cancer, but it *will* take some pressure off your immune system simply by reducing your stress, and this may help restore your clarity and sense of agency.

Ideally, we'd all resolve our key childhood traumas *before* getting sick. An ounce of prevention and all of that. But it's especially important for our recovery. Even if it doesn't provide a cure, tapping will almost certainly bring a greater sense of peace. Death of the body is inevitable and best met with a calm and peaceful heart.

CHAPTER 35

The Parent-Child Relationship

Being a parent is arguably the single most important job on the planet, and yet there are no requirements whatsoever. No license. No exam. There's not even a suggested list of qualifications. What other career can you enter accidentally?

There's an idea in psychology of the 'good enough' parent. There are no perfect parents, all of us have personal issues. But if Mom and/or Dad are good enough, if they can provide enough interest, love, compassion, respect, and attention for their children then *attachment* can happen. And that means their kids have a fighting chance of having a good life.

Attachment is a really big deal. As baby mammals, we need to bond with our parents, both physically and emotionally to feel safe and develop a sense of belonging. For infants and very small children, Mom and Dad provide the template for *all* people. Life in the family becomes our template for the whole world.

There's a certain baseline feeling of being safe, wanted, important, protected and loved that all of us need. We either get this from loving parents or parental figures who care for us or else we don't.

Many wonderful parent education books are available today – *How to Talk So Kids Will Listen and Listen So Kids Will Talk* by Faber & Mazlish and *Positive Discipline* by Jane Nelsen are two of my favorites. Dr. Sears has some great books on 'attachment parenting' for new and expecting parents. This knowledge can really help us be 'good enough' as parents.

But what if it's too late? Your kids are grown and you've already messed them up. Well, as long as you feel guilty, I guess it's okay, right?

Parental Guilt

I've noticed a cruel irony in my work with clients. The kindest people, the ones who are really trying to do right by others and make the world a better place, these are the people most inclined to feel guilt. The very ones who least deserve it. At the same time, by all accounts truly evil sociopaths feel no remorse whatsoever!

For parents though – the ones who really want to be better than 'good enough' – guilt over parenting mistakes is actually a very destructive thing. For the good of their children, it needs to be tapped away. Let me explain.

Parental guilt means feeling bad that some mistake we've made has impacted our child. Somehow, we've failed them, and so we feel bad about ourselves as parents. This is really coming from a place of wanting to be better, to do better. It's a sign of our ultimate good intentions, and so the guilt may actually register as a good thing. It's not.

For the child, their experience is that *when Mommy looks at me, she feels bad.* And of course, that's true. Our children tend to be hyper-aware of our moods. They totally notice when looking at them makes us feel bad. They don't understand we're feeling bad about ourselves. To the contrary, they *know* that it's their fault. And in a rather sad way, they may be right.

When we're feeling guilty as parents, what we're really doing is comparing our actual kid with some idealized fantasy version of them in an imaginary world where we never messed up. And our fantasy kid is doing a *lot* better – they're happier, more secure and confident, more successful, getting better grades, they're doing great! By comparison, our real kid kind of sucks. Hence the guilt.

Indulging in parental guilt means we're projecting disappointment onto our kids. They see it in our eyes and take it very personally. They don't understand that we're blaming ourselves, and it wouldn't matter if they did. We clearly feel bad when looking at them, so obviously they're not good enough. They may not know exactly what it is, but they know for sure that something must be wrong with them.

Can you see how destructive this is? Parents I work with on this issue often have a terrible moment of realization where they feel guilty about feeling guilty! It's like a guilt fractal! After tapping though, this distress becomes serious determination to release the guilt and start regarding their kid with appreciation, gratitude, and faith that they'll actually turn out okay.

Forgiving ourselves is mandatory if we really want to be good parents. Our kids chose *us*. There was no mistake. Even if something really bad happened and it really *was* our fault, they knew before incarnating exactly how fucked up we were, and what sort of wild ride that would give them. It's important to have high standards for ourselves as parents, and just as important to model self-love, self-forgiveness, and self-compassion.

Even if your kids are adults now, making this shift can take a lot of subtle (or maybe not so subtle) pressure off your relationship with them. However, it's not enough to simply 'get' this intellectually. Really making the shift will probably require some EFT tapping, to get the limbic brain on board.

Monsters

Unfortunately, some of my clients had parents who were absolutely NOT good enough, to put it mildly. Growing up they experienced abuse and/or neglect from their primary caregivers. In terms of severity, there's definitely a continuum. On the slightly less destructive end are parents who were simply reenacting their own childhood abuse by unconsciously taking on the role of the parent-abuser. This can happen unintentionally and automatically.

I remember when my first daughter was around two years old, and she did something naughty. Suddenly I heard my father's words coming out of my mouth with exactly the same harsh tone of voice! I was absolutely shocked. It was like an exact recording had been switched on without any awareness on my part. The words were out before I knew it and all I could do was apologize after the fact. By way of silver linings, I learned that day how healing a sincere apology can be for a child.

I'm guessing this experience of automatic replay is nearly universal for parents. Scolding is one thing, but if the 'recording' includes heinous verbal, physical or sexual abuse, healthy attachment will be seriously compromised. And apologies are rare indeed, given the walloping dose of shame that's usually present.

I've noticed that reenactment tends to split along gender lines. This is by no means universal, but as a general rule boys often grow up to take on the role of perpetrator, while girls are more likely to stay in the victim role and find someone else to play the part of the abuser.

On the other end of the *not good enough* parent continuum, things are much scarier. These parents go way beyond merely reenacting their own abuse. They *intentionally* try to damage, possess or destroy their own child. There's speculation that traumatic brain injury may play a part in this. Whatever the cause, I think of these parents as criminally insane, though they often present well to the outside world. This is truly the stuff of nightmares.

About five years ago I decided to shave off my beard just for a change, and I was surprised to discover deep frown lines etched around my mouth. Where the hell did those come from?! I quickly realized they were caused by my natural empathic expression (a sad frown) whenever I'd hear some terrible story. I grew my beard back.

On the next page, in no particular order, I have a short list of some of the *not good enough* parents I've encountered working with my clients:

the Satanic cult member
the narcissist
the borderline personality
the alcoholic/drug addict

the schizophrenic
the sexual predator
the rageaholic bully
the chronically depressed
the suicidal drama queen
the stone cold unreachable one
the sexaholic/workaholic/anything-aholic
the disappearing parent who never came back

It's no joke growing up with a parent who matches even one item on this list. Even worse when both parents do. And for a true horror show, how about both parents matching multiple items? I've worked with clients who grew up that way, but it doesn't mean they're doomed. Not at all. But it's likely to take a whole lot of work to recover their sense of self and safety in the world. Thanks to EFT and Matrix Reimprinting, it really *can* be done.

CHAPTER 36

Romantic Relationships

Have you ever had a crush on someone? It can be pretty intense! And when a crush gets reciprocated, watch out! There are few drugs more potent than falling in love. And few experiences more devastating than breaking up.

According to Carl Jung, what's really going on here is projection. The object of our affection seems so perfect and wonderful because we're actually projecting our own idealized inner feminine/masculine archetype onto them. Jung called these archetypes the Anima (the perfect feminine) and Animus (the male counterpart). But honestly, the whole thing is a dirty trick!

It's a dirty trick because it's totally doomed from the start. Eventually, our projection wears thin, *guaranteed*. We start to see glimpses of the real person underneath and even if they're actually pretty great, they're never going to be that glorious perfect divine being we thought they were. It's just not possible.

In other words, our rosy-pink-bubble is going to pop. Sooner or later reality sets in. If we're wise to this dynamic, we might let it go gracefully and allow real love a chance to develop. If not, we're apt to blame our partner (*"You've changed! You're not the man I married!"*) then bail on them, hoping that next time 'love' will last.

Selection Error

Addiction/recovery specialist Terry Gorski once said the number one relationship problem is selection error. Sometimes people laugh when they hear that. It *is* kind of a grim joke. Gorski is basically saying that we tend to choose wrong partners and most relationships are pretty much doomed from the start.

I'm sure Mr. Gorski was really on to something, but I don't believe it's a selection *error* at all. We evaluate and select potential partners with uncanny precision. Or rather our subconscious mind does this for us. It just has different goals than ours.

Romantic relationships are the perfect venue for reenacting childhood traumas – those we experienced directly, and the second hand ones, we witnessed our parents going through. Our new partner is almost always a stand-in for Mom and/or Dad.

Meeting someone who will serve us in this way provides a curious kind of excitement. Ironically, another suitor might be hanging around who would make a genuinely awesome partner. They're loving, loyal, intelligent, successful, and would make a great parent – but they register subconsciously as 'boring', unable to provide the needed drama. This is a cruel irony, and I've had many clients who deeply regretted rejecting such a person.

Alas, their subconscious mind had other fish to fry.

When we're growing up, our parents' relationship (or lack of one) becomes our template. The way they did it is the only way to do it. And no matter how uncomfortable or unhappy it was, anything else feels alien and doesn't quite fit. For some people, being happy and content for too long can actually generate real anxiety!

As children, if we witnessed fighting, or abandonment, or cheating, or one partner was an addict, an enabler, a belittling critic or long-suffering martyr, or one parent was volatile and terrifying, or cold and emotionally unavailable – our subconscious will find just the right partner to reenact these traumas.

Sometimes it's not really marriage problems we're reenacting, but rather our direct relationship with one of our parents. Maybe Mom and Dad got along great, but you were Mom's scapegoat and suffered terrible verbal abuse. Chances are you'll find a partner to carry on the scathing.

Remember, the purpose behind all of this reenactment is resolution. The subconscious is trying to get those traumas out of your system in the only way it knows how – repetition. Unfortunately, this strategy rarely works. Maybe it never works. Instead, repetition tends to reinforce our negative beliefs – this really *is* all I can expect from partnership.

Of course, this whole thing totally sucks. At some point, you might make a solemn vow to *never* put yourself through something like that again. If Dad and the last three boyfriends were rageaholics, you'll find someone *safe* for once. A guy who never even raises his voice, who actually has no access to his anger whatsoever.

At first, this might seem wonderful. *Finally,* it feels safe to be in partnership. What a relief. But often something weird starts to happen. Your milquetoast partner starts driving you crazy. He's a doormat! He's spineless! His limitations become intolerable, and eventually *you* become the angry partner. You may end up reenacting the same abuse dynamic, but this time as the perpetrator!

Then again, sometimes we're tricked. Dad was a total deadbeat, so you find someone super successful. He's really good with money and has an awesome career. Then six months in, through no fault of his own, he loses his job and just can't find a new one. He feels so bad about letting you down, maybe he starts drinking. So now you're leaving for work, and he's lying on the couch in his pajamas, binge-watching Netflix.

Abracadabra, you married your father! No *way* could you have seen that coming. But your subconscious did.

So how do we change this? Can we really hack our way out of this dysfunctional relationship reality? Yes, and I have two tapping exercises below that you can do right now! Skip ahead if you like, or stay with me and we'll take a look at the painful low ebb of romantic relationships – the breakup.

Recovering from a Breakup

Few things are more devastating than the end of a significant relationship, especially if we're the one getting dumped. The feelings can be absolutely overwhelming and our thoughts totally obsessive. It's hard to find any peace, and sometimes our physical health can really suffer. While the terrible intensity does fade over time, our experience of relationships may be sadly tainted, leaving us bitter and sometimes scared to start over.

The good news is that EFT can *dramatically* speed up our recovery and takes us way beyond just 'getting over it' by releasing old patterns, setting us up for a massive upgrade in our next relationship. This is one of my favorite issues to help clients with, and over the years I've noticed there are basically three stages.

First, we have to deal with the raw emotions – hurt, anger, sadness, guilt, anxiety, regret, and despair are common. Even if the breakup happened years ago, there might still be a lot of intensity just below the surface. It's amazing how quickly these feelings can be discharged, even with simple basic tapping.

Next, we go after the most common negative beliefs that almost always show up after a painful breakup, running like a horrible tape loop in our head. Often we're haunted by the belief that "This was my last chance for being loved." And, often there are add-ons such as "...and I blew it" or "There will never be anyone like _____ again" or something like, "Once he saw who I really am he ran away."

The remedy is to simply tap through the points while declaring those statements as if they're totally true. As you continue tapping I pretty much guarantee they'll sound increasingly absurd, especially having already discharged the most intense emotions.

Another terrible belief to tackle is, "I can't trust myself – I didn't see that coming." "He got in under my radar – I couldn't protect myself so what's to keep it from happening again?" "My only choice is to never date again and suffer desolate loneliness or face the certainty of having my heart destroyed again!"

These ideas may actually seem true when we're still reeling from the breakup. After a few rounds of tapping on these statements, I like to throw in a few new ideas: "...and I learned *nothing* from that experience. My radar hasn't improved at all, in any way. I'm exactly the same person who fell in love with him in the first place. I'm just older, not wiser. I'd make exactly the same decisions again."

The absurdity of these statements rapidly undermines our doom and gloom narrative. In an almost startling way, what seemed *so* true and tragic suddenly becomes silly, almost comical. The dread of starting over may even be replaced with the first twinges of excitement – it will be different, and better, next time.

The third stage of breakup recovery is a bit more involved and hinges on the answer to the question, "Who was my ex standing in for?" or, "Who does he remind me of?" Look at your ex's bad behavior, the things they did that really upset you, where have you seen that before? It's usually pretty obvious in hindsight, and usually Mom or Dad.

So this third stage of recovery is about resolving the key childhood traumas we've been reenacting with our partners. To some extent, this can be done with EFT, but working with a skilled Matrix Reimprinting practitioner is ideal. Either way, the exercises below may jump start this process.

Relationship Tapping Exercises

1. Removing Friction: Think about your current partner (or ex) and make a short list of the top 5 to 10 things they do that just bug the hell out of you. Perhaps they're always leaving a wet towel on the bed, or never put gas in the car. Or maybe it's something more serious like being harshly critical or drinking too much.

Taking one list item at a time, tune into how upsetting it is for you right now, on our zero to ten scale. Tap on whatever feelings are coming up and every aspect of how that thing bugs you. See if you can get the intensity down to zero, or as close to zero as possible. The tapping may bring up related memories from childhood. If so, tap away whatever negative intensity the memory brings up for you.

It may take a few days or even a week, but tap through every item on your list. You may notice after doing this that, without you ever saying a word about it, your partner actually stops doing whatever it was that bugged you. This can be just a little spooky, but enjoy it!

And if you're currently single, tapping through your list means your next partner is likely to be an awesome upgrade. Give it a try!

2. Relationship Beliefs: Read through this lovely list of relationship affirmations and note how true each statement seems for you, on a 0 to 100% scale, where 100% means it's absolutely true for you.

_____ It is safe for me to love

_____ I am loved for who I really am

_____ What I want wants me

_____ My needs are important and valid

_____ I am taken care of

_____ I take good care of my relationships

_____ I am emotionally available

_____ I am good at healthy boundaries

_____ I am sexy

_____ Someone thinks of me during the day and smiles

_____ My vulnerability is my strength

_____ My heart is full

_____ I am attractive and attracting love

_____ I am seen and I am heard

_____ I can relax and enjoy my relationship

_____ I can trust myself and trust my partner

_____ I am whole and complete no matter my relationship status

_____ I am open to deep connection

_____ I am perfectly imperfect, and my partner loves me for that

_____ I am adored for all my quirks

_____ I am so grateful for my soul mate

_____ I'm attracted to a partner who sees me as an equal

_____ I'm attracted to a partner who wants the best for me

_____ I'm open to a healthy, loving relationship

Special thanks to Steph Dodds for these affirmations

If any of the statements are especially false for you, let's tap on them. This is an interesting way to use EFT that often shifts our level of belief simply by tapping on the statement itself. It's also kind of fun.

Since EFT works best by tapping away what's wrong, let's frame each affirmation in a negative way. For example:

Tapping on the karate chop point:
Even though it's just not true that _____, I deeply love and completely accept myself.

Then just keep refuting the affirmation:

Tapping through the points:
It really isn't true that _____."
I wish _____ was true but it's totally not.
Wouldn't it be nice if _____, but that's just not the case for me.

You might be wondering, why not simply tap on the affirmation itself? Why keep saying it isn't true? Again, we're actually doing is tapping away whatever blocks we may have to genuinely, accepting the statement. Trust me!

Just do four or five rounds of this, tapping through the points, and then check back in with yourself: Does the statement seem more true? Has your zero to 100% rating changed? I know it's weird, but I've done this exercise with hundreds of students, and it almost always works great.

If distressing memories surface while tapping on the affirmations, see if you can tap your intensity down to zero for each one.

Imagine if you could tap each affirmation up to 100 percent – how might your life change? Honestly, even a small improvement is bound to help your outlook. So what are you waiting for? Give it a shot!

CHAPTER 37

Procrastination

Grace described herself as stuck. She'd been working with an awesome business coach and had developed a clear vision and course of action for building her ideal business. But mainly she was just doing crossword puzzles and hating herself.

Just thinking about all the time she'd been wasting gave her such a bad feeling that after tapping a bit I had Grace ask out loud. "Show me an image of my younger self who is really feeling this way." The scene that popped up showed her 15-year-old younger self sitting at the dining room table late at night struggling over her algebra homework.

Grace told me she just never did *get* algebra and barely passed with a D., and she only got a D because the teacher felt sorry for her. He could see how hard she was trying. I had Grace imagine stepping into that late-night homework scene to help her younger self.

It turned out Dad was also in that scene 'helping' the 15-year-old by standing over her and yelling about how stupid she was. Dad had often hit her in the past, one time actually knocking her unconscious! Apparently, dad was a total math whiz. He thought his daughter was just being stubborn, refusing to learn something that was obviously easy to understand.

The poor girl was terrified of him and absolutely stuck in fight or flight. No wonder she couldn't do the math!

So, we tapped on the 15-year-old and got her calmed down. She was going through a rough patch in her life for a lot of reasons – her grandmother had recently died, and they'd been very close. Her family had actually moved into Grandma's house, so there were daily triggers for her grief.

And moving meant she'd had to start a posh new high school mid-year and felt like a total loser. She didn't have nice clothes and felt like a hick. And of course, Dad's abusive bullying definitely wasn't helping! She'd actually done pretty well with regular arithmetic in earlier grades when her life wasn't on the skids.

After tapping on the 15-year-old, we also tapped on Dad – validating his feelings of frustration but helping him see that his efforts were totally counterproductive. He was able to disengage and go listen to music.

What we did next was a little weird. Did you ever see *The Matrix?* In that film, it's possible to download information for someone through a jack in the back of their neck. Information like knowing Kung Fu, or how to fly a particular helicopter. So Grace and I simply downloaded algebra into the 15-year-old (*Matrix* style through the back of her neck), bypassing all of her blocks so she would just know it.

As soon as the download was complete, the 15-year-old started cranking through her math homework like the problems were simple puzzles. She was ecstatic! Grace was blown away witnessing this and asked me, "Does this mean *I'll* be able to do algebra now?" That question kind of blew my circuits! I honestly had no idea.

You're Not the Boss of Me

So what did any of this have to do with Grace's procrastination? Now she'd do algebra problems instead of crossword puzzles?

Here's what Grace and I pieced together. At least part of the 15-year-old's problem with math was about getting back at Dad. She wasn't going to let him bully her and win. He was actually right when he called her stubborn! She was stubbornly refusing to knuckle under to him. Her doing well in math would be Dad winning.

Dad is long gone now, but every time Grace would try to push herself to complete an assignment from her business coach, she was essentially taking on the role of her dad. She even felt some of the same feelings toward herself that he used to express – frustration and contempt!

This would absolutely trigger her younger selves locked in a battle of wills with Dad. Remember, our younger selves don't know who *we* are. They're trapped in their own time and place. But Grace's determination to force herself to get something done was somehow registering with them and activating their resistance.

As we worked, Grace realized she actually *was* acting like her father, in subtle or not-so-subtle ways. This realization was hard for her to take. But we all take on attributes of our parents by osmosis, right? It's a thing.

This awareness was very helpful for Grace. She was intensely motivated to stop being "Dad" and to find a way to get her younger selves on board with accomplishing new things, to enlist their aid.

The Roots of Procrastination

I have a great photo of a little girl, arms crossed over her chest, glaring at an adult just off-screen. All you can see of the adult is their admonishing wagging finger. It's easy to read the little girl's thoughts: "You're not the boss of me."

I think a great deal of our procrastination comes from an inner child stuck in this attitude of defiant rebellion. They're confusing us with their parent!

When I decide to get up half an hour earlier to meditate or to stop eating wheat, or go to the gym, I'm making that decision from my grown-up, adult perspective. It may be all about self-care and self-love, but I'm essentially stepping into a parental role with myself.

If I happened to grow up with a demanding, critical or domineering parent, there's a good chance my well-intentioned decision will activate a whole posse of younger selves. I'm unknowingly invoking a massive power struggle—one that I'm likely to lose.

Other reasons for procrastination might involve feelings of deep inadequacy – instead of rebellion, there's an intense fear of exposure by the younger self. Failure seems guaranteed, so why risk everyone finding out how worthless I am by trying something new?

There can also be anxiety around losing one's place in the family system, especially if we're living out the role of the black sheep. If I try and actually succeed somehow, I won't fit in anymore. There may be real fear of being abandoned or rejected.

Again, our younger selves don't know we exist. They don't know who we are. But our decisions to take some kind of positive action can trigger their resistance, and this may be the root of most procrastination.

Don't Put This Off!

If procrastination is a big problem in your life, exploring any childhood roots might be a lot more helpful than doubling down on the old willpower or beating yourself up.

Here are a few simple questions to get you going:

Did I have an overbearing parent?

Was there an endless to-do list of chores?

Was whatever I did just never good enough?

Did I have a perfect sibling who could do no wrong?

Was I forced to become a caretaker for a parent or my siblings?

Is there some humiliating failure or defeat I've just never gotten over?

Answering yes to any of these questions suggests you have at least one younger self-causing your procrastination.

Try making a list of memories related to your answers above. Choose one to work on right now (yes, right now – you don't want to procrastinate, do you?) Choose the one that has the most emotional charge when you think about it.

On a scale of zero to ten, how much intensity does that memory give you right now? And what sort of feelings? See if you can tap the intensity down to zero for each memory, one at a time. It may take a little while but stick with it. Eventually, your procrastination may be a thing of the past – literally!

Hacking Reality exists only because this EFT stuff really works. The evidence is here before you. All throughout the long process of writing this book I've had to tap away my own layers of resistance and procrastination. Tapping has helped me 'get myself out of the way' enough to allow these words to flow through me.

On a final note, I checked back in with Grace about a week after our session. She told me that as soon as we'd finished, she went online and found algebra problems to download. She spent hours doing them just for fun! But after that, she got right to work on her business!

CHAPTER 38

Hacking Reality for Others

W hat if the biggest problem in your life is actually someone else?

Maybe your own life is going along nicely, but a loved one is struggling with serious emotional or health issues. You're worried but feel powerless to help. Or you have an evil ex apparently dedicated to messing with you. Custody issues and child support payments are just a venue for revenge.

Perhaps your child is struggling. She's 15 and burdened with crippling social anxiety. Or, he's 44 and moved back in with you – eight months ago! And no sign of an exit strategy. What can you do?

In the old paradigm, we're all just separate individuals with limited ways to connect. You could try talking with your loved one, maybe stage an 'intervention'? I suppose if that doesn't work you could pray for them. Hey, maybe you could pray that your evil ex gets struck by lightning? That doesn't always seem to work.

In our new paradigm though, there's something that often does work. It's called Surrogate Tapping.

Thanks to the magic of quantum entanglement, our strong emotional connection with our problematic other person actually provides access to help them.

Even if we pretty much *hate* them (the evil ex comes to mind), our overall approach in surrogate work is focused on helping them – the idea being that if they weren't so messed up, they wouldn't be messing with us. If we can bring love, perspective, encouragement, and light to someone in a dark place, perhaps they can make better choices.

This ain't Voodoo

The intention of surrogate work is always to alleviate suffering rather than manipulating behavior. Even if we *are* hoping to change a behavior (wouldn't it be nice if the baby on your flight stops screaming?) it's still all about helping that person release emotional distress.

While surrogate work is *always* done for the benefit of the other person, it's rarely done with their knowledge or permission. The obvious ethical question here is, "Don't you need someone's permission to help them?"

It's a good question. Let me answer it by asking another question – do you need permission to pray for someone? For example, if you came across a terrible car accident would you feel free to pray for the welfare of the people involved? Or would you actually have to go and ask them first?

I've asked hundreds of students that very same question in my EFT workshops. Nearly all of them said they wouldn't hesitate to pray in those circumstances. Whether one believes in the effectiveness of prayer or not, either way, there's a sense that it's harmless and benevolent by its very nature.

Surrogate tapping can be seen as a highly focused form of prayer. If you *do* feel you'd need permission to pray for someone, then surrogate work is probably not for you.

Voodoo, at least the way it's portrayed in the movies, *does* attempt to manipulate behavior, overriding free will. Casting a spell to get someone to fall in love with you is clearly unethical. And laying a curse on someone, whether it actually works or not, is seriously bad karma. And that's *not* what we're up to with surrogate tapping.

Fate vs. Free Will

Although it's very rare to ask consent from the recipient (it's just not practical in most cases) I always ask their higher self, picturing a traffic light that's either red or green.

I'm not worried about meddling with someone against their will. On the contrary, I don't believe we can help someone against their will so it would be a waste of my client's time and money if, on the Soul level, the recipient wasn't receptive.

And some people aren't. If their suffering is part of the Soul's plan to learn something, gain empathy, cancel out a karmic debt or whatnot, then that's that. Whatever they're going through *feels* destined to happen, it's their fate.

It feels that way, but really we use our *free will* to arrange our own fate, but we do so *before we're born* and of course, we don't remember. That doesn't mean we can't change our mind though, once we're here. Especially once we've learned whatever we came here to learn.

If someone *is* amenable to changing their 'fate', then surrogate work is a great way to help them make that kind of shift.

Do It Yourself

If you'd like to try surrogate work to help a loved one, I have two different methods for you. Before you try it though, it's best if your emotional connection with the recipient is as clean as possible. That means tapping away any strong negative feelings you might have toward that person or their situation – resentment, anger, guilt, anxiety or fear, even deep sadness.

All of these feelings create turbulence so tapping can help you get yourself out of the way. Once you've achieved a relatively calm and neutral state, check out the techniques below. Both can be very effective, but one might suit you better.

The Channeling Approach

Here you simply tap as though you actually *are* the recipient, taking on their negative emotions and thoughts by bringing them into your own body. Usually, you'd close your eyes and just start with a set-up statement:

Tapping on the karate chop point:
Even though I, Skippy the dog, am so scared by all those loud noises in the sky, I know my master will protect me, and I'm a good dog.

And then, tapping through the points say all the feelings and aspects that seem to come up:
those terrible booms
those bright lights in the sky
it's so scary
I just want to hide under the bed and never come out
It's so loud and scary
but I know my master loves me
I know she'll take care of me
all of this fear....

And yes, you can do surrogate tapping for dogs, horses and other animals. It works great!

Taking on the energy or persona of someone else can be intense if they're having a really hard time. It might take many rounds of tapping until you get a sense that they're feeling calm, peaceful, content or even happy.

You might wonder whether you're just making it all up. My advice is don't worry about it. If you're invested enough to actually try helping someone, you probably have a strong enough connection for the tapping to work. That said, speaking just from my own experience, it's *very* clear when I start to actually channel someone. And just as clear when the tapping has worked for them.

It might be tempting to call the recipient right after you've tapped, and ask if they feel any better. Given how weird that might be for them, I'd suggest you proceed with caution. But if you're in a position to hear of any changes, hold onto your hat. This stuff can really work!

The Matrix Approach

Here you imagine stepping into a scene where you can tap directly on the recipient. You might picture yourself stepping into their kitchen and tapping on them as they are right now. Or the scene might be a memory, in which case you'd step in as you are right now and tap on their younger self there.

Before stepping in, freeze anyone else in that scene to stop the action, so to speak. Go to the recipient, take their hand, and let them know you're there to help. Ask them what they're feeling, what's the matter?

Begin tapping on them, saying words that address whatever is wrong. And everywhere you tap on them, it helps to tap on yourself in the same places. Depending on what's wrong, you might say something like:

Tapping on the karate chop point:
Even though you're so angry right now, and you have this bitterness toward your family, I know you want to be a good person. You want to be happy.

Tapping on the points:
All this anger
All this bitterness
you can't believe how you're being treated
it's so unfair
they never listen to you
no one ever takes your side
you must feel so alone right now
so angry
all this anger toward your family...

This approach works best if you can 'allow' the recipient to be real as if some part of them really is showing up to do the work with you.

When you ask them "What are you feeling?" or, "What's going on for you right now?" taking a mental step back and allowing *them* to respond is ideal. Their answers may actually surprise you.

Don't get hung up on whether this is real or not. Even if it seems like you're just making it all up in your head, so what? Go ahead and do the tapping anyway. Keep checking in with them and tap on any new feelings that come up. Just keep going until they feel a lot better.

For Real?

This whole idea might seem really stupid. But then the dog next door stops barking. The baby on the plane stops screaming and goes to sleep. Your brother is on the phone, apologizing! How is that even possible? Your son gets a great job offer and OMG, he's *finally* moving out! Your evil ex drops the lawsuit.

I'm still astonished when surrogate tapping works, even though it pretty much always does. Quantum entanglement is for real. We really *are* connected in the Matrix, so why shouldn't we be able to leverage our connections to help others? Einstein called it 'spooky action at a distance' and it pretty much freaked him out. But hey, if electrons can do it, we can too! After all, we're pretty much *made* of electrons!

Wait, What About Saving the World?

I teach surrogate work in my workshops, and every so often someone gets really excited about saving the planet.:

"Hang on, can we use this on the President?!"
"What about tapping on business or political leaders so they won't destroy the Earth?!"
"Can we use this to stop war?"

You can certainly try. You certainly wouldn't be the first to make an attempt. I'm sure there's no harm in it, but I have my doubts you'll succeed. Here's why.

Both methods of surrogate tapping I've presented work best when we have a strong but clean emotional connection with the recipient. I believe this reflects the strength of our quantum entanglement with that person. And connection implies a two-way street.

You may have *very* strong feelings about the President of the United States, but does he even know you exist? There's probably not a very strong connection or entanglement there. Another problem here is that anyone we know of *only* through media channels may be very different than who we think they are. Our feelings and intentions may be directed towards an artificial image, rather than an actual person.

Then again, maybe it's worth a shot! Just be aware of that slippery slope of trying to manipulate behavior, rather than simply alleviating suffering. Stay away from the voodoo dolls!

None of us can see the whole picture unfolding from our own limited human perspective, but a stance of love and compassion is always safe and helpful. If you'd like to try saving the world through EFT and Matrix, more power to you!

CHAPTER 39

Hacking Your Money
Mindset

What is your relationship with money right now?
Are you comfortable with your income? Do you have
enough coming in to meet your expenses and then some?
Do you have a nest egg? A bit of savings set aside?

Does a nice windfall show up time to time? Is there an easy flow of
money into your life, with an overall feeling of financial security?

Or are you stressed out? Struggling with debt? Do you have to
work *really hard* to earn every penny? Are you plagued by financial
insecurity no matter how much you make?

Not that long ago I was in the totally stressed out category,
working way too hard and never making quite enough. I went
through a stressful period of juggling credit card balances and
suffering through the hopeless feeling that can bring.

And maddeningly, if a windfall ever did show up, like an
unexpected check from my grandmother, there would *always* be
some emergency expense to cancel it out. The car would need a
repair, or we'd have to take the cat to the vet. My financial thermostat
was set pretty low.

All of that has changed for me. Today I rarely think about money.
It's basically a non-issue. Not that I'm a millionaire (as of this writing
anyway). But I do have plenty of income, *and* I love my work. I can
take time off when I want or need to, and I feel financially supported
by the Universe.

Let's see if we can get you to this same sort of relaxed, wonderful place. As you may have gathered by now, it's all about beliefs.

Believe It or Not

Most of us have a real mixed bag of financial beliefs we've adopted from our families, religious influences, school, friends, and definitely advertising and the media. As little kids we just soak these ideas up like sponges, unable to question whether they're true or not.

Often our money beliefs actually conflict with one another, which can create real problems for us – indecision, self-sabotage, bad luck and getting really stuck. Our money beliefs affect how optimistic, satisfied and grateful we feel (or don't feel), how big our goals will be, how comfortable we are giving and receiving, and the settings on our 'financial thermostat'.

Acting as perceptual filters, our money beliefs *definitely* color how we experience what's happening to us. For example, it's easy to miss opportunities when we're not expecting or looking for them. Or if we feel deeply suspicious and guarded when they do show up.

But could it be that opportunities are less likely to actually show up for us if we're running negative money beliefs? That we're not just overlooking them, but somehow keeping them away? I've seen this in my own life and for so many clients who've cleaned up their money beliefs - they get an unexpected raise or promotion, the lawsuit gets dropped, business picks up, a fantastic new idea shows up, there's a sudden windfall.

Positive thinking 'think and grow rich' style books go back at least one hundred years, proliferating in modern times. Personally, I really like them and have a few classics on my bookshelf. But I've come to believe that EFT tapping has always been a missing and essential ingredient in Law of Attraction work.

And it does take some work to change our beliefs. It's just a lot easier and vastly more productive than 'good old-fashioned elbow grease' or nose-to-the-grindstone efforting.

Reprogramming Your Beliefs

I've assembled a collection of both negative beliefs and positive affirmations about money and wealth. As you read through these lists, please rate how true each statement seems to you, using a zero to 100% scale, where 100% means absolutely true, and zero is totally false. This is sometimes called the *Validity of Cognition scale*—or VOC for short.

Don't overthink your VOC number! Let's keep your rational mind on the back burner here. Honestly, whatever number first comes to mind is probably the best one to use. In other words, how true does it *feel*? We're not so much interested in Universal Truth here, it's more a question of how true the statement is for you and your life right now? You might consider jotting down your numbers as you go through this list.

The statements in the first list are negative, limiting beliefs. A low number for these is great, and a high number means trouble! For the second list of affirmations, it's just the opposite. It would be great to believe all of them 100%. Low numbers mean serious pessimism around money.

Once you've gone through both lists, choose just one statement to start with. You can simply start at the top, or pick one that seems important, where a change might really make a difference for the better. Don't worry, over time you can do them all, but this process works best if you do one at a time.

Limiting Money & Wealth Beliefs

How true are these statements for you? Please rate each one on a scale of 0 to 100% (*where 0% is completely false, and 100% is absolutely true*).

_____ Money doesn't grow on trees

_____ Time is money

_____ Nothing in life is free

_____ Money is the root of all evil

_____ Rich people are a bunch of greedy snobs

_____ I can't get ahead because the economy is bad

_____ Success is hard work, and I don't want to work that hard

_____ It's lonely at the top...everyone will be jealous or judge me

_____ I'm too _____ to succeed (old, young, uneducated, fat...fill in the blank!)

_____ I don't have enough education to be successful

_____ It's more spiritual to be poor

_____ I don't have what it takes to be successful

_____ It's not what you know it's *who* you know, and I don't know anyone

_____ I can't handle money

_____ Everything is too expensive

_____ There's not enough to go around—if I win someone has to lose

_____ Spiritual people don't care about money

_____ It isn't safe to do too well—something bad will happen

_____ It's not okay to want more, that's being selfish and greedy

_____ It's not okay to make more money than my father/mother/siblings

_____ Why bother? I'll just have to pay more taxes

_____ It takes money to make money

Money & Wealth Affirmations

How true are these statements for you? Please rate each one on a scale of 0 to 100% (*where 0% is completely false, and 100% is absolutely true*).

_____ I can make all the money I need doing work I love

_____ I am rich and prosperous

_____ It's safe, fun and easy to make lots of money

_____ I am worthy of a wealthy life

_____ I am open to the best things in life

_____ It's safe for me to focus on making money

_____ I am debt-free as money is constantly flowing into my life

_____ I always have more than enough money

_____ The more I receive, the more I can give

_____ I am wealthy right now

_____ I receive and accept money with love & gratitude

_____ I am a rich child of a loving Universe

_____ I love money and money flows easily into my life

_____ It's okay to have more money than I need

_____ It's okay for me to have more money than other people

_____ There is more than enough for everyone

_____ Everything I put my hand to prospers and succeeds

_____ My rich blessings in no way interfere with anyone else's good

_____ Everyone wins when I succeed

_____ It's safe for me to get excited about money

_____ It's safe for me to make money easily

_____ I'm comfortable with my success and know who I am around successful people

Time for Some EFT

Once you've decided on one belief statement to start with, let's do some tapping. If you haven't tried EFT yet, please visit Chapter 20 for the EFT Crash Course.

For the negative beliefs, you can just repeat the statement over and over, saying all or part of it for each point. After 2-3 rounds of this, try elaborating on the statement, playing with the wording, maybe exaggerating a bit, or focusing in on some aspect of the statement that has the most emotional charge.

See the example below for inspiration.

If a memory comes up while tapping, make a note of it. Perhaps it's where you first took on the belief or some emotionally intense incident that gave the belief special importance. At that point, you'll want to take a break from tapping on the statement and do some tapping on this memory.

The trick here is to notice what feelings come up just thinking about the memory and how intense they are now, at this moment, on the EFT zero to ten scale. Simply tap on those feelings as you tune into that memory and try to get the intensity of the emotion as close to zero as possible. Once the emotional intensity around the memory is down, check back for the statement VOC.

Tapping for the Positive Money Affirmations

EFT works best by tapping away *negativity*, so instead of saying the positive affirmation while you tap, I suggest framing it in a negative way:

"Even though it's not true that _____."

"Even though I'd love to believe that _____, I know it's not true for me."

"Even though there's no way in hell _____, I sure wish it was true."

Again you want to tap until your VOC number changes significantly for the better, as close to 100% as possible.

Check out the example at the end of this chapter for ideas.

Do You Believe in Magic?

Do you know this saying?

Life isn't happening to you, life is responding to you.

That may be hard to believe when you're putting out a lot of effort and intention, and things still don't seem to go your way.

Here's the problem – life is mostly responding to your feelings and expectations. These have the strongest impact *by far* on what you're attracting. That's why EFT can be *crucial* for making positive belief changes. Tapping releases the old, stuck feelings that hold our beliefs rigidly in place.

Often when we're tapping on a negative belief, it starts to seem absurd! Maybe our VOC level was really high, you totally believed it, but suddenly that belief is just ludicrous. That's probably because we were very young when we decided it was true. Even the smartest kids draw some incredibly dumb conclusions – they simply lack knowledge and experience.

If you can tap the VOC on a negative money belief down from 80% to 30%, that's likely to have real-world consequences for you. Get it down to 0% and your life may really start to open up. *This is where the magic really happens!*

And the tapping doesn't take very long - maybe ten to fifteen minutes for each belief or affirmation. If you commit to doing one or two beliefs a day, you could work through both lists in a month. Try setting a timer for ten minutes. Just keep tapping until it dings, then check the VOC. Still too high? Tap for another five minutes. Lather, rinse, repeat.

Negative Statement Tapping Example: Money Doesn't Grow on Trees

Set up statement on the karate chop point:
"Even though money doesn't grow on trees, I deeply love and completely accept myself."

Tapping around the points:
Money doesn't grow on trees
you can't just go out and pick it like fruit off a tree
it's hard work making money
you have to work and work to get it

money doesn't grow on trees
money isn't low hanging fruit
there's no way you can just go out...
and pick it off a tree
money doesn't grow on trees
the only way to get money is work for it
and work hard for it
no one is giving it away
no one ever just gets money
it doesn't just fall from the trees like apples
money has to be worked for
money doesn't grow on trees
but I guess I did get money for my birthday that time
my Grandma used to give me money
my friend did buy me dinner that time
but still
money doesn't grow on trees
it's true it's made from paper...
which does come from trees I guess
but it's hard to make money

And so on. Once you get going, just keep on talking about the statement. Perhaps set a timer and tap for 5 minutes or so. What will this do for you? A lot of our negative beliefs are actually pretty flimsy. Even simple tapping like this can reduce your VOC. *And the less you believe your statement is true, the less it will limit your experience of life*. It really is that simple.

Affirmation Tapping Example: I Can Make All the Money I Need Doing Work I Love

Set up statement on the Karate Chop point:
Even though there's no way I can make all the money I need doing work I love, I still deeply love and completely accept myself.

Tapping through the points:
There's just no way I can make all the money I need doing work I love

I wish that was true for me, but it's not
I can't make that much money doing work I love
I'd love to believe that was possible, but I know it will never happen
I can't make all the money I need...
doing work I love
it just doesn't work that way
no one is going to pay me to do what I love
you have to do unpleasant, difficult things to make money
I mean, maybe I could make a tiny amount of money...
doing work I love
but not enough to live on
no one can do that
no one can make a living doing what they love
that's just not possible
okay, well maybe some people have figured that out
or maybe they're just lucky
but not me, I can't make all the money I need doing work I love
if I loved my work, I'd be happy
no one gets paid for being happy
no one wants to hire someone to work for them who isn't miserable
everyone hates their job or business
no one can actually love what they do and get paid for it
that's basically just having a hobby you like – no one will pay for that
there's absolutely no way I could ever make money doing work I love
or at least not enough money
but what if I could?
I'd sure love to be wrong about this idea
I choose to open my mind up to the possibility I could actually make
all the money I need doing work I love!

Will this practice *really* change your life? There's only one way to
find out. Go for it!

CHAPTER 40

Conclusion

By now I hope you have a sense of how possible it is to change your life by hacking your reality. I'm not saying it will be easy, necessarily. It still takes work, but with the tools and mindsets I've shared here, that work can be incredibly productive. Let's review some of the highlights covered in this book that can help you hack your own reality:

You are a Soul. You're inhabiting this current body and personality, but you've had many lifetimes. In order to fully immerse yourself in the reality of this lifetime, you've chosen to forget all the others for now

Your life isn't just happening to you. You were born into circumstances and relationships designed to provide specific opportunities to grow. You actually *planned* this crazy ride before you were born and then chose to forget your choices. Amnesia is the price of admission to Earth school.

There are all kinds of things you signed up to learn and experience, but you have the option of 'testing out' of any lessons you'd rather not learn the hard way. Probably the best way to do so is to actually 'get' the learning, rather than deferring it. Matrix Reimprinting is the tool of choice for this.

Because on the deepest level of reality all time is happening now, it's totally possible to go back and help our younger selves who are frozen in moments of trauma. Helping them is a powerful way of revamping our belief systems and perceptual filters, which profoundly changes our current experience of life.

Your body is made of subatomic particles winking in and out of space. It feels solid and stable and real, but fundamentally it's just energy coalescing into the morphic blueprint that is you. Whatever physical problems you're experiencing are likely caused by static (unresolved traumas), interfering with the perfect expression of that blueprint.

Sometimes clearing up those traumas can manifest an immediate return to perfect health. Sometimes there are so many traumas it might take a bit longer, but you don't have to do them all. Once you reach a tipping point, it's a downhill ride.

The quickest and easiest way to remove traumatic static is through EFT, which hacks into our limbic brain, communicating directly with the amygdala there and turning down the volume on stress and switching off Fight or Flight. Tapping can remove our triggers and discharge old stuck emotions.

EFT is the closest thing we have to a panacea (our motto is 'try it on everything'), and it just happens to be easy to learn and easy to use. I strongly suggest using it daily as regular emotional health hygiene.

If weight issues are a major preoccupation for you, we've covered various ways of getting down to the real issue that weight is a solution for. Common themes are protection from unwanted attention, fear of deprivation, 'winning' a power struggle at all costs and the fear of isolation. An ounce of tapping equals a pound of dieting – or ten pounds, more likely!

As adults, our most troublesome relationships are most likely reenactments of childhood traumas. Your subconscious mind has an uncanny knack for choosing just the right players to stand in for Mom or Dad or other key figures from your childhood. The motivation is for healing and resolution, but it's a primitive strategy that doesn't work very well for humans. In fact, it tends to backfire, reinforcing our negative beliefs.

Luckily we can now heal our original traumas directly, with EFT and Matrix Reimprinting, which means we no longer need people to show up and reenact them for us. Relieved of this task, the worst people in our life either become a lot nicer or just go away, to be replaced by nicer folks. Either way, we get an upgrade.

As you begin shedding old stuck emotions, negative beliefs and the dramas of reenactment, your ability to manifest health, success and creative self-expression will progressively increase. In other words, life is going to get a lot better for you.

There are a great many wonderful things to do here on Earth, once you've freed yourself up from so much of that learning through suffering business. Developing genuine affection for this place may actually be one of the final requirements for graduation.

As long as you *are* here, it's a really good idea to check in and identify your deepest dreams, desires, and goals, making sure they're really yours and not just implants from family, society or the media. You have enormous inherent power to manifest whatever reality you most desire. The entire Universe is rooting for your creative self-expression!

I hope that *Hacking Reality* has opened your eyes to some helpful new ideas and strategies and that it continues to be a resource for you. EFT and Matrix Reimprinting can truly be your new best friends. If you are interested in working with a skilled practitioner, which is a great idea if you have some serious trauma to resolve, you'll find suggestions in the resources section in the back of this book.

Keep up the good work and let me know how it's going if you like. I'd love to hear about your miracles.

Special Request from Rob

If you've enjoyed reading Hacking Reality, I would greatly appreciate a short review on Amazon or your favorite book website. Reviews are absolutely crucial for any author, and even just a line or two can make a huge difference. Thank you!

Resources

Stay in Touch with Rob:

Hacking-Reality.com
Let's keep the ball rolling! Updates, articles, and events.
TappingtheMatrix.com
Gateway to working with Rob, plus videos and articles.
TappingtheMatrixAcademy.com
Interested in becoming an EFT/Matrix practitioner?

Further Reading:

The Lazy Man's Guide to Enlightenment
by Thaddeus Golas. This book is a short, elegant and entertaining primer on practical metaphysics.

Illusions by Richard Bach
One of my all-time favorite spiritual books – so good!

The Biology of Belief by Bruce Lipton
Liberation from genetic determinism through the cutting edge science of epigenetics. Truly essential information.

Transform Your Beliefs Transform Your Life by Karl Dawson & Kate Marillat. A great introduction to Matrix Reimprinting, packed with useful insights.

Journey of Souls by Michael Newton
What are we up to between lifetimes? Read this book to find out!

8 Keys to Brain Body Balance by Dr. Robert Scaer
Fascinating information on the Freeze Response, Trauma Capsule & more.

The Body Keeps the Score by Bessel Van Der Kolk
One of the great classics for understanding emotional trauma.

Science Set Free by Rupert Sheldrake
Fairly mind-blowing stuff – a much needed antidote to Scientism.

The Sense of Being Stared At by Rupert Sheldrake
Why shouldn't science address the really trippy stuff people are fascinated by?

For Your Own Good by Alice Miller
Alice Miller takes us down into some very dark childhood territory. A sad, but ultimately liberating trip.

Thou Shall Not Be Aware by Alice Miller
Not really for the faint of heart, but powerful good stuff to know.

Bradshaw On: The Family by John Bradshaw
This book is densely packed with indispensable psychological insight

The Field by Lynne McTaggart
A complete and total classic.

The Divine Matrix by Gregg Braden
Actually, any or all of his books are great…

The Michael Handbook by Jose Stevens & Simon Warwick-Smith. A good primer on the Michael Teachings which I've found very useful.

Find a Practitioner

Certified EFT Practitioner Directory
These are some of the best practitioners out there.

Low-cost EFT Clinic
Highly trained student practitioners getting their certification hours offer absurdly low-cost sessions.

Index

amnesia 10, 20, 26, 35, 109, 271
amygdala 100, 101, 272
attachment 187, 188, 233, 236
autoimmune disorders 219

blue tit 72, 73

cancer 2, 21, 86, 225-231
classical mechanics 41, 45
core belief 93
Craig, Gary 5, 149, 281

Dawson, Karl 5, 116, 119, 162,
   275
dissociation 18, 109, 110, 121,
   134, 135, 219, 226

ECHO 118-121, 176, 182, 219,
   222
EFT 2, 4, 39, 99-101, 114-117,
   125, 136, 139, 141-149, 159,
   186, 190, 193=195, 206, 221,
   231, 235, 237, 242-245, 250,
   254, 259, 262, 265-267, 272-
   273
Einstein, Albert 11, 45, 46, 52,
   56, 57, 137, 170, 258
entheogens 26
epigenetics 1, 2, 81, 83, 84, 225,
   275

fibromyalgia 219-222
Fight or Flight 4, 97-101, 104-
   107, 118, 133, 222, 247, 272
Freeze Response 2, 81, 101-109,
   113-115, 118, 119, 133, 136,
   171, 176, 214-216, 219, 222,
   276
Freud, Sigmund 30
future self 193-196

genetic determinism 83-86, 275
grief 108, 178-181, 185, 230, 248
guilt 169, 170, 177-180, 234,
   235, 242, 255

hacking 3-6, 9, 33, 53, 55, 59, 70,
   79, 83, 95, 116, 126, 139, 199,
   205, 209, 250, 253, 261, 271
hypnogogic state 92, 128
Jung, Carl 30, 49, 239

karma 37, 39, 169, 170, 172, 186,
   254

Leibovici, Leonard 58-59
Levine, Peter 104, 105, 108, 115
limbic brain 99, 100, 105, 107,
   142, 235, 272
Lipton, Bruce 85, 87, 99

Mandela Effect 64-66
Maslow, Abraham 123-125, 129
materialism 12, 31, 47-49, 51, 53,
   85-86
Matrix Reimprinting 2, 4, 5, 11,
   59, 80, 115-118, 121, 136,
   159, 161, 195, 213, 237, 243,
   271-272
Michael Teachings 36, 37
morality 52
morphic field 69-70, 72, 74-75,
   78-79, 114, 134, 216

Newton, Isaac 41, 43-46, 48, 69,
   209
Newton, Michael 21, 178

old soul 37-39

panic attack 110-111, 145
parallel universes 63, 66
past lives 167-171
Peoc'h, René 51
perceptual filters 5, 114, 154,
    188, 262, 271
procedural memory 109, 115
procrastination 90, 171, 193, 247-
    251
psyche 29-30, 113, 134-135
psychology 29-33, 48, 233

quantum field 55, 57, 79, 133
quantum mechanics 45, 52, 57,
    61, 80

random chance 51-52
reenactment 106, 113, 116, 122,
    133-136, 163, 189, 236, 240,
    272-273
retrocausation 59, 61, 81, 185
reverse engineering 131, 134, 136

Scaer, Robert 107-109, 112
Schrödinger, Erwin 60
self-actualization 123, 129-130
Sheldrake, Rupert 44, 48, 56, 57,
    70, 74
spirit guides 40-41
spirits 48, 176, 178-181, 196
subconscious 10, 30, 89-91, 94-
    95, 106, 109, 112-116, 122,
    132-135, 144, 188-189, 196,
    207, 209, 215, 227, 240, 241,
    272
superposition 60-61, 79, 81, 195
surrogate 162, 253-259
synchronicity 49

The Field 13, 55, 56, 70, 77-81,
    161, 195, 211, 213
trauma capsule 107-115, 118,
    121, 133-134, 189, 215-216,
    219

Ushers 21

ABOUT THE AUTHOR

Rob Nelson holds a Masters in Counseling Psychology and is an ordained minister in the Universal Life Church. He spent most of his early career working with traumatized children and teens, and teaching parent education classes, as well as staffing the 'graveyard shift' for a suicide prevention hotline.

Rob encountered EFT in 2007 and Matrix Reimprinting in 2011, becoming certified as a practitioner and ultimately Master Trainer for both techniques. He was trained and certified in EFT by Gary Craig, the original creator of this modality.

As the founder and director of Tapping the Matrix Academy, Rob now trains, mentors and certifies practitioners in EFT and Matrix Reimprinting. He is one of only 4 Matrix trainers in the US and Canada.

In addition to training and mentoring, he maintains a private practice with clients worldwide. Married since 1985, Rob has two grown daughters and makes his home in Santa Rosa, California.